OUR FATHER...

DISCOVER THE MAP TO THE GREATEST TREASURE

GEORGE MATHEWS, MD

Published by Carpenter's Son Publishing, Franklin, Tennessee
Edited by Gail Fallen
Front cover image by Jorge Cocco
Cover and Interior Design by Debbie Sheppard
ISBN 978-1-956370-06-5
Printed in the United States of America

ACKNOWLEDGMENTS

I am most thankful to my Lord for revealing to me what a masterpiece the prayer that Jesus taught his disciples is. I also thank and attribute to the Holy Spirit the prompts for me to write this book, as well as for His guidance all through the process.

I am grateful to my wife, Letha, for her love and patience, especially during the months that I worked on this manuscript. I particularly appreciate her encouraging confidence in my writing even before reading what I wrote.

My special thanks to my children, Nikhil and Anita, (whom I still consider as children, though each of them is often a far more discerning adult than I). Despite their busy schedules and though they live in another state, they have pored through my manuscripts, provided valuable feedback, and suggested corrections and refinements, for which I feel indebted.

This book is also the product of countless sermons that I have heard from pastors, preachers, and lay leaders, in person, over the radio, television, and online, not to mention the very many books and passages that have illuminated the teachings of the Bible over the years.

Let me also take this opportunity to express my gratitude to the many thousands of patients over nearly five decades who allowed me the privilege of delving into their lives to understand the predilections of the human mind and the choices we make.

I also wish to acknowledge the patience, guidance, and encouragement of my publishers, Larry Carpenter and Shane Crabtree, whose efforts helped this book see the light of day.

G.M.

CONTENTS

PREMISE

The Bible recounts man's alienation from God after an idyllic beginning. Created with the ability to choose, man (inevitably) made choices contrary to God's instruction. That damaged man's filial relationship with God. More importantly, the Bible presents the path to the restoration of that relationship through God's offer of reconciliation. Even though man breached the relationship, God (through Jesus) bore the sacrifice to redeem man and established a new covenant. Jesus restored man's access back into God the Father's family and His Kingdom. Man's ability to make choices still remains. Man still gets to choose whether or not to avail of the access that Jesus provides. And whether to abide by his understood will of God. Some do; some don't.

When we opt for restoration, communion and fellowship with the Father is reestablished. We remain error-prone. But, through the forgiveness afforded by Jesus's sacrifice and the guidance of the Holy Spirit, we can receive course corrections to get back on the "narrow" road and be delivered into the Father's Kingdom. Deliberations on this prayer, which Jesus taught his closest followers, outline how this can be accomplished.

Most Christians memorize this prayer at a young age before appreciating its significance. This prayer continues to be read / recited regularly by tens of millions every week, though few pause to recognize the treasures therein. Let us bask in the light of this masterpiece, which was actually taught by "the Master," and be shepherded on our path to salvation and sanctification.

PREFACE

A few years ago, I was confined to bed for a couple of weeks following surgery. During that period of physical inactivity, particularly when I would wake up in the middle of the night, I wanted to channel my thoughts profitably. I felt led to spend more time in prayer, because my prayer times had previously tended to be rushed and had suffered from easy distraction.

I recalled reading about the disciples asking Jesus to teach them to pray. I felt that would be a good place for me to start too. I was very familiar with the prayer that Jesus taught his disciples, having memorized it more than fifty years earlier and having recited it thousands of times. I had expected to be done with it in short order. But meditating on the Lord's Prayer took me to soul satisfying depths that both thrilled and surprised me. I had found a treasure trove. It consumed my weeks of recuperation. And it continues to keep me absorbed in the years since then. More importantly, I discovered what I and several fellow believers who I have talked to had been oblivious about. Through this prayer and its elaboration, Jesus had imparted both his gospel message of salvation as well as the essentials of sanctification that follow salvation.

I was accustomed to people (including myself) uttering long-winded prayers, after which the Lord's Prayer would sometimes be recited by way of completion or a finishing touch. I can honestly say that, each day now, after meditating on the Lord's Prayer, I feel fulfilled and replenished in my personal prayer times. All that I previously used to pray about is captured in this soul-nurturing prayer. Dwelling on this prayer continues to open up new vistas for me, which I credit to illumination by the Holy Spirit. I have continued to gain fresh insights into this prayer, even during the writing of this book.

This prayer, recorded in the sixth chapter of the Gospel of Matthew (and also in the Gospel of Luke) consists of just five verses. But the deliberations on them draw on scores of additional Bible verses, which lend context, amplify, and intertwine within the tapestry of this prayer. I have attempted to capture in this book the additionally realized meaning and significance that I had failed to recognize in over fifty years of my previous familiarity with it.

Prayer occurs in the realm of our mind and spirit. As a psychiatrist, I have included some personal insights into the functioning of the mind as it pertains to the teachings in this prayer.

Some time ago, I came upon a question on social media that intrigued me: "What would you like to leave to your grandchildren that you consider valuable?" Not having any grandchildren of my own then or now, I didn't labor that particular angle (except to prod my children about it). But the question as to what one prizes the most has stayed with me. I have asked myself what I would like to leave to anybody dear to me that I considered of lasting value. I concluded that I treasured the soul-satisfying richness of the Lord's Prayer the most, and that is what I have tried to present to the reader in this short book.

Since this is the prayer that Jesus taught his disciples, these meditations are addressed primarily to those who desire to be closer followers of Jesus. I also offer it to those who may be content with the state of their relationship with God but remain open to scriptural edification. It could particularly benefit those at risk of reading or reciting the Lord's Prayer without recognizing the treasures therein. I additionally hope that any one unfamiliar with Jesus, what he was and is all about, will find in these pages a reliable (though necessarily incomplete) presentation of Jesus's invitation and offer to all mankind.

Though this is popularly called the "Lord's Prayer," it is really the prayer that the Lord taught his disciples to pray. It has therefore also been referred to as the "Disciples' Prayer."

If I ever were to have grandchildren, I hope they would read this someday and be blessed by where God's Spirit leads them. For you, the reader, my sincere hope is that you discover previously unidentified treasures in this prayer, as I have. I hope it provides you hope, joy, peace, and enlightenment like it has for me. We believe that the scriptures were inspired by the Holy Spirit. We have the priceless advantage of having that very same inspiring author present with us while we read the scriptures to provide illumination and clarification. May the Holy Spirit reveal to you further insights in the course of this exploration, and may you exult in your own reflections on this prayer.

GEORGE MATHEWS, MD
BRENTWOOD, TENNESSEE

INTRODUCTION

The Gospel of Luke records that the disciples asked Jesus to teach them to pray. The disciples had been drawn to this charismatic person, who was compassionate and performed many miracles of healing. His teachings were authoritative, compelling, and thought-provoking; sometimes, they were even confounding. Jesus said he was empowered by God, who he claimed was his Father. He wanted everyone to know about his Father and his Father's Kingdom. They further observed that Jesus spent much time alone in prayer, communing with his Father. That seemed to be of utmost importance to him.

As disciples, they observed him and learned from him. They were not scholars, and, though he was called "rabbi," his teaching was not of the typical rabbinic style. Most of his instructions were through practical demonstrations of interactions with real people who struggled with a variety of burdens.

After a period of discipleship, which we might consider a live-in internship, Jesus sent his disciples out (on a practicum?) to nearby villages. They were tasked with doing what they had seen Jesus do: spread the good news about the Kingdom of God being at hand and to heal the sick. When they did, they were amazed that they too had been empowered to heal some people, though some others seemed beyond their ability to help. When those persons, whom the disciples were unable to heal, were brought to Jesus, he healed them easily. And, when asked, Jesus told the disciples that it took prayer to effect healing like that (see Mark 9:14–29 New International Version).

Since the disciples were his innermost circle of followers, they asked him to teach them how to pray.

Jesus responded, saying,

"This, then, is how you should pray:

'Our Father in heaven,
hallowed be Your name.

Your kingdom come;
Your will be done on earth
as it is in heaven.

Give us this day
our daily bread.

And forgive us our debts,
as we also have forgiven our debtors.

And lead us not into temptation,
but deliver us from the evil one."

MATTHEW 6:9–13

Wow! Was that the master key that opened any and all locks? Would the incantation of those few words, infuse the disciples with superhuman abilities and power? Clearly not! Over the millennia since then, billions of people have recited that prayer without it usually seeming to effect any appreciable change.

Furthermore, recitation of that prayer could be done in less than a minute. Yet Jesus himself was reported to have spent many hours at a time in prayer. So, clearly, there was more to prayer than the utterance, audibly or otherwise, of certain words.

We all have learned to pray from others. Our family members, friends, community elders, or others who have influenced us have shaped the form and content of our prayers. We may have borrowed phrases (or even portions of prayers) that others have prayed, if that resonated with us. Prayer, though, often tends to be reduced to supplications. It is comparable to a wish list presented to God, who, we want to believe, could be persuaded to shape the future favorably for us. When we listen to prayers, ours or others', we find that much of the content often consists of attempts to inform God or to instruct Him on what we want Him to do. If and when those prayers seem to repeatedly go unanswered, we get discouraged. We may conclude that prayer is not as effective as we might wish it to be. But, in times of desperation, many still turn to prayer as a last resort—a last ditch effort, when nothing else has worked. An American football metaphor is that of a "Hail Mary pass" (from the favorite Catholic and Orthodox prayer which begins with "Hail, Mary ..."), a desperate, long throw by the trailing team in the final seconds of the game, with equal or greater chance of failure, when no other option seems more likely to avert the loss.

But that is not what prayer is. God is not our personal genie. Prayers are not the means for Man to bend God's will.

Prayer, in its essence, is to align ourselves with God and His will!

Desktop printers, when they were new, or when new ink cartridges were put in, required (it's optional now) the user to print out a test page with lines, shapes, and colors. The user was then prompted to scan that page to determine whether the alignment was perfect. Prayer, similarly, is a time to "scan" our perceptions, desires, and will to see if it aligns with God, as revealed through His word and His Spirit within us. In so doing, we receive revelation, correction, redirection, and peace. There is no greater peace than the assurance of being in synchrony with God's will in our lives.

One of my math teachers used to say that two triangles are congruent only when they would perfectly overlap with each other. Prayer is our means to seek congruence with the will of God.

This prayer that Jesus taught accentuates the gospel (good news) of salvation and leads us along the path of sanctification, while steering us toward the will of God. Sanctification is the process of being transformed from who we were to who God wants us to be. Can we really get all that from this prayer? There's one way to find out. Let's explore it and see.

Jesus repeatedly preached, "The Kingdom of Heaven is at hand" (Matt. 4:17). He was figuratively holding out his hand, to say, "I'm here to invite you into my Father's Kingdom. I'll show you how you can get there." And that is what this prayer effectively does. If we have a desire for the Kingdom of Heaven, Jesus (through the Holy Spirit) undertakes to equip (sanctify) us to get us there.

But before Jesus taught his disciples how to pray, he first instructed them on how *not* to pray. The first point Jesus made was that we are not to pray so as to impress anybody else.

"When you pray,
do not be like the hypocrites,
for they love to pray ... to be seen by others."

MATTHEW 6:5

Jesus also emphasized that using long prayers or flowery speech was futile. He told his disciples that

"Your Father knows what you need
before you ask Him."

MATTHEW 6:8

If God the Father knows our needs and knows our thoughts, then what is left for us to pray about? That's what we are about to discover.

In 2021, Drs. Chan, Moses, Ganguly, and Metzger, along with their research and clinical associates at the University of California, San Francisco, made a remarkable breakthrough that they call "speech neuroprosthesis." They developed a program called BRAVO (**B**rain Computer Interface **R**estoration of **A**rm and **V**oice) which enabled a paralyzed person, unable to speak or move, to communicate, by transcribing his brain signals.[1] Humans have finally discovered ways, with the help of very sophisticated instruments, to decode and transmit the thoughts and intentions in another human's mind, with his cooperation.

This is, undoubtedly, a very significant milestone in neuropsychological science. But it is also theologically significant because it helps us begin to appreciate how God perhaps hears our unuttered prayers. This is also just a few tantalizing steps removed from understanding how our God could perhaps have spoken things into being!

I hope you sense the awe as we step into the awareness of our God's realm through prayer. Lead on, Holy Spirit!

Jesus taught this prayer to his closest disciples. This prayer was principally for those willing to follow him and heed his instruction. Jesus provided his disciples access to his Father and his Father's Kingdom. He invited them to be the first to live out the good news: "The Kingdom of my Father is at hand and available to you."

Jesus additionally urged his disciples to extend this invitation to anyone else who was willing to truly follow him to become his disciple (Matt. 28:19–20).

CHAPTER 1

Our Father in Heaven

"Our Father ... "

The beginning of the prayer that Jesus taught his disciples is probably familiar to billions of people. Many can follow through with some or all of the remainder of the prayer by rote. But familiarity often causes us to skim over the multilayered richness of its content. I invite you to savor the immense treasures in this prayer in small morsels. Let us start with the very first word in this salutation.

Our: a possessive pronoun, plural. "Our" signifies that something or someone belongs to us; that is, to me and to at least one other person, possibly many, or even all persons. Jesus taught this prayer to his disciples, perhaps as a collective prayer, but he also instructed them to pray alone and in private, as recorded in a verse preceding the teaching of this prayer.

> *"But when you pray,*
> *go into your room,*
> *close the door*
> *and pray to your Father,*
> *who is unseen."*
>
> MATTHEW 6:6

So could Jesus have wanted his disciples to be mindful of any other persons when we pray alone and say, "*Our* Father"?

Let's broaden our perspective.

Around the world, the term "God" is sometimes a nebulous concept. It is used to refer to the infinitely great power, way beyond our limited comprehension, who keeps the universe (or multiverse) going. The world that we live in has existed long, long before our time and will probably exist long after our time as well, if we discount some reports of impending cataclysms. Looking at the night sky, we are amazed at the billions of stars strewn across a canopy of mind-boggling distances. A visit to an observatory amplifies that realization manifold. And something keeps these celestial bodies in their positions. At the other end of the spectrum, looking through a high-powered microscope, we can see very minute cell organelles that keep the building blocks of life functioning in what are undoubtedly masterpieces of dynamic equilibrium.

Though man sees himself atop the food chain here on earth, he invariably recognizes that something/someone infinitely superior to him orchestrates the world in which he lives. Through human history, individuals, communities, or nation states acknowledged the orchestrator of the universe and ascribed names to refer to that notional entity, with "God" being a generic title.

In his book *Natural Theology: or, Evidences of the Existence and Attributes of the Deity*, William Paley used the analogy of an intricate watch. Marveling at the intricacy of the watch would lead us to infer the existence of a watchmaker. The implication then, is that the orderly complexities in our world would suggest the existence of a world maker.[2]

Some cultures gave names to their Gods: *Amun-Ra* of the Egyptians, *Brahma* of the Hindus, *Zeus* of the Greeks, *Jupiter* of the Romans, *Ahura Mazda* of the Persians, etc. *Allah*, the Arabic term for "God" is used by Muslims around the world. Some cultures would not name their God but, instead, referred to their God by titles. That is like how we refer to royalty, using honoring titles like "His Excellency" or "Her Royal Highness." Likewise, we respectfully refer to religious leaders with titles like "Your Holiness" or "His Grace." Similarly, God was referred to by many titles.

The Jews referred to God as *J-H-W-H*, (Lord God / the self-existing one), but would not utter that name. They also had other titles like *Adonai*, (LORD), or *Elyon*, (God Most High). Sometimes He was referred to by His attributes, like *El Shaddai*, (God Almighty); *Jehovah Jireh*, (Lord God who provides); *Jehovah Rapha*, (Lord God who heals); etc.

Into that Jewish environment came Jesus, who consistently referred to God as his Father. Even "Father," the English translation, sounds rather formal. He referred to God as "Abba," which is more like "Papa" or "Daddy." That level of claimed intimacy with God divided his listeners. Some who witnessed his actions, teachings, and power over nature accepted him as "Son of God." Others considered him a charlatan, an outrageous blasphemer, and even a devil, deserving of being put to death. The main ones who wanted Jesus to be put to death were the priests and religious leaders who took offense because they saw themselves as the only ones authorized to instruct the people in all matters relating to God. To them, Jesus was challenging their rigid traditions that had been established ever since Moses led the Israelites out of Egypt. How *dare* this untutored Galilean usurp their role. Jesus also disrupted the religious profiteering that took place and exposed the duplicity of the dogmatic Pharisees. They were determined to make him pay dearly.

Now, two millennia later, this same question is put to us too. Who do we say Jesus is? See if any of these descriptions sound familiar: Itinerant preacher given to exaggeration / misquoted or misunderstood sage/con artist/mentally deranged person/a man about whom a legend was fabricated/truly the Son of God the Father?

Accordingly, each of us also has a decision to make. Is Jesus for real? Is what he said true? Do we need to heed what he said?

It is understandable that some may want more information to help them make that choice. Others may even ask whether they need to make a choice at all. Does it matter if they remain undecided? Here's why I believe it matters: This decision determines our enduring identity, our destiny and our permanent citizenship.

One of the exercises I give my patients and students to work on, to address self-identification and purpose, is to write a page on "Who am I? Why am I living?"

Most people think they know themselves well but struggle to come up with more than their roles, relationships, and station in life when they attempt to put down the answers on paper.

In most of what was recorded in the gospels about him, Jesus talked more about his Father and His Kingdom of Heaven than on any other subject. One of Jesus's earliest statements, as he was reading from the scriptures while in the synagogue in Nazareth, was

"The Spirit of the Lord is on me because
He has anointed me to proclaim good news . . ."

LUKE 4:18

The good news that he repeatedly proclaimed was that the Kingdom of Heaven was at hand. Mankind had pondered about Heaven since the beginning of time. Some considered it a figment of imagination. Jesus, though, claimed that he came from Heaven. And now, Heaven was being made accessible to the common man. In real time. By Jesus. Through Jesus.

Jesus's message was that he had come to invite us all into the family of God, His Father. He was figuratively offering a ticket to his Father's Kingdom in Heaven. That ticket was free. As we shall see a little later, Jesus would be footing the bill. He would pay the price for that ticket with his life—through his death.

He entreated his listeners, saying in effect, "Believe that my Father in Heaven sent me. Come into our Kingdom as my brother or sister." Believing that could be the difference between our life ending with our death on earth or continuing to live with him in his Father's Kingdom, even after we die here.

In his first epistle, John the Apostle concluded emphatically that

"Whoever has the Son has life;
whoever does not have the Son of God
does not have life."

1 JOHN 5:12

As it particularly applies to us, John also added,

"Yet, to all who did receive him, to those who believed in
his name, he gave the right to become children of God."

JOHN 1:12

That is significant because it addressed believing in Jesus

as the deciding factor that determines our identity: whether or not we get to belong to the family of God. And our citizenship: Are we merely citizens of one of the countries on one of the continents on a small planet where we will perish, or are we citizens of the Kingdom of Heaven, where we will get to live forever?

Jesus said,

> *"The one who believes in me*
> *will live,*
> *even though they die."*

JOHN 11:25

Though some may choose to dismiss this claim, if true, it is really a matter of life or death, even more so than our life here on earth.

Jesus made an even more pivotal claim when asked about the way to his Father's house:

> **"I am the way, the truth,**
> **and the life.**
> **No one comes to the Father**
> **except through me."**

JOHN 14:6

That is probably the most audacious sounding yet profound exclusive-inclusive statement ever. Nobody can come to the Father except through Jesus! Yet anybody who wants to come to the Father is welcome—through him. Having the label of "Christian" is not a prerequisite. Nor are having lived a pious life or having performed any religious rituals. Not even a good life. No resume required. No prerequisites at all.

Realizing that we cannot get there by ourselves but accepting Jesus as the way to the Father and His Kingdom (like the thief on the cross did) is all that is needed!

Life on earth was believed to end on earth. Everyone born had a shot at a season of life. Whenever it was over, that was the end. But Jesus's mission was to make known that life, even after it ends on earth, could continue in his Father's Kingdom, eternally. Jesus demonstrated that by rising up from the grave after his own death. That offer is now available to any and all who wish to accept it. But Jesus offers the only bridge to his Father's Kingdom.

Jesus also assured them that all are welcome:

"Whoever comes to me
I will never drive away."

JOHN 6:37

This prayer that we are studying was taught by Jesus to his disciples. They were called by him, walked with him, talked with him, and having witnessed everything he did and taught, they believed that Jesus was indeed the Son of God.

When asked, while many others struggled to figure Jesus out,

"Simon Peter answered,
'You are the Christ,
the Son of the living God.'"

MATTHEW 16:16

In the millennia since then, billions of people who never saw Jesus nor heard him speak have also accepted that Jesus is the Christ and the Son of the living God. Many did so nominally, because their parents or others who were influential believed so and taught them to believe likewise. But some did so because there stirred within them a quest to connect deeply with the true, living God. And that yearning was only met through Jesus.

When we accept Jesus as the Son of the living God, we too find ourselves on the *way* to God the Father with Jesus. But that is just the beginning of the journey on which this prayer takes us.

Significantly, Jesus is also the way to the Father and His Kingdom in prayer. As believers in Jesus, we don't pray to a physical God who appears before us, nor to any image or structure designed to represent Him. We pray in spirit, because

"God is spirit . . ."

JOHN 4:24

We come into the presence of God the Father with the assurance that Jesus, God the Son, our "intercessor," vouches for us. Our invitation is from Jesus the Son to use his access to the Father. For without Jesus, we have no justifiable standing with God the Father.

When I pray, I personally find it very encouraging and comforting to imagine the presence of Jesus, invitingly saying, "Come, let's talk to **Our** Father. The Holy Spirit will tune us in."

Remember that it was Jesus's death that tore the veil that had previously kept the Holy of Holies inaccessible (see Matthew 27: 50–51). More on the significance of Jesus's death in chapter 6.

When I accept Jesus's invitation to join his Father's family, his Father becomes my Father and, likewise, the Father to all who so believe. Hence, he is *our* Father.

But how do we interact with God the Father? We do so through the agency of the Holy Spirit, who is our assigned "helper" and "counselor," sent to us by the Father and Son.

> *"And I will ask the Father,*
> *and he will give you another helper,*
> *to be with you forever . . ."*

JOHN 14:16

The Holy Spirit is God Himself, spiritually extended to us. He deciphers our thoughts and inaudible prayers with a spiritual form of the speech neuroprosthesis,[1] outlined in the Introduction. The Holy Spirit can perhaps be imagined as a live superconductor who transmits God's presence to us and relays the utterances of our souls to Him.

Jesus is the *face* of the Father. Not in physical appearance, but in terms of the Father's nature, compassion, and character.

The Holy Spirit is our *interface* with the Father. The conduit for us to interact with the Father.

Our ability to utilize this interface requires time and practice, with prayer being the principal means. So prayer is our communion with the Triune[3] God—Father, Son, and Holy Spirit—at the same time.

Let's look at yet another aspect of prayer.

Our culture grooms us to be individualistic . . . to a fault. Our individualism sometimes leads us to overlook the collective context in which we have our physical and spiritual existence. Each of us exists as one among many. We often forget that we are part of a larger whole, even among those accepting adoption into God's family.

Our belief is that Jesus came as the Messiah to be our Christ (Savior) and to redeem us to eternal life in his Father's Kingdom. That belief also leads us to believe that He will come again.

"And if I go and prepare a place for you,
I will come back and take you to be with me
that you also may be where I am."

JOHN 14:3

Will he be coming again just for me or just for you?

No. We believe that he will come again for all who have believed in him. We collectively are the "Body of Christ," the "Bride of Christ," for whom he will come again.

"Now you are the body of Christ
and individually members of it."

1 CORINTHIANS 12:27

If we are collectively one body, we pray not only as individual "cells" of a body but also *as* the whole body and *for* the whole body. Any time we pray, there are always others praying with us, unbeknown to us, to the same Father, through the same Holy Spirit. That larger context of belonging to the "Body of Christ" lends added meaning to the term "*Our* Father" as we explore the remainder of this prayer.

"*Our* Father"

Here's an understandable question, especially for those who may be relatively new to seriously exploring this prayer. How do we address God as our Father when we have never set our eyes on Him, nor ever audibly heard His voice, let alone never having felt His physical touch? Let's see what Jesus had to say about that.

The Gospel of John, chapter 14, records the disciples struggling with this very issue. They asked Jesus to show them "The Father." Jesus responded by saying,

> *"Anyone who has seen me*
> *has seen the Father."*

JOHN 14:9

Jesus also said,

> *"I and the Father are one."*

JOHN 10:30

The apostle Paul further reinforced that,

> *"The Son is the image of the invisible God,*
> *the firstborn over all creation."*

COLOSSIANS 1:15

But what about us who did not even get to see or hear Jesus in person? Jesus had an answer for that too.

As he told his disciple Thomas, who had refused to believe that Jesus had risen from the dead until he saw Jesus with his own eyes and felt him with his hands.

"Because you have seen me,
you have believed;
blessed are those who have not seen
and yet have believed."

JOHN 20:29

This is where faith steps into the picture and plays a major role. Our invitation into the Kingdom of God is undeserved. That is grace! Unmerited favor. That grace is the result of the amazing, incomprehensible love of Jesus (and God the Father) for us while we were undeserving of any such sacrificial love.

"For God so loved the world
that he gave his only begotten Son . . ."

JOHN 3:16
NEW KING JAMES VERSION

Our acceptance of that love and grace is by faith. We believe, by faith, Jesus's assertion that he was truly sent by God, his Father, to invite us into his Father's Kingdom and family.

"For it is by grace that you have been saved, through faith —
and that is not from yourselves,
it is a gift of God —"

EPHESIANS 2:8

Even our faith is a gift from God! Faith prompts us to connect the dots when not everything is objectively proven. How great is His love for us that he invites us into His family, not because of who we were or are, but because of who He sees us capable of becoming transformed into, in Jesus Christ? He even gifts us the faith to accept that!

Jesus himself encouraged his followers to accept the Kingdom of his Father:

"Do not be afraid, little flock, for your Father
has been pleased to give you the kingdom."

LUKE 12:32

It is worth appreciating that early (see 1 Peter 1:3 and 1 Corinthians 11:31) church leaders, including the apostles Peter and Paul often referred to God as "the Father of our Lord Jesus Christ" and He still is for us. Jesus came as the Son of God the Father. He encouraged us to also accept God as our Father. We may struggle to reach that level of intimacy with God when we previously had a very formal, distant, and reverential view of Him. (I recall the awkwardness when my professor first asked me to call him by his first name. I felt more comfortable addressing him by his title.)

When we believe Jesus to be the Son of God the Father, his Father becomes our Father too, and we become His children.

Please note that though we haven't seen Him, He has seen us and *continues* to see us.

"The eyes of the Lord are on the righteous,
and His ears are attentive to their cry."

PSALM 34:15

"For You created my inmost being;
You knit me together
in my mother's womb."

PSALM 139:13–14

King David wrote the above Psalm some three thousand years ago. It was only in the 1950s that James Watson and Francis Crick discovered the double helix structure of DNA.[4] The recognition that the specific *knit* of the genes on our chromosomes determined our biological characteristics also came about in the twentieth century. And it is now known that the determination of the specific genes that populate the twenty-three chromosome pairs for each of us took place in our respective mothers' wombs.

It can take man millennia to discover the ways of God.

It is fascinating and awe inspiring to consider that God the Father, through so many generations of our ancestors, had been selecting the particular genes with which to knit us long before we or even our parents were born. That could provide us the answer to the question: Are we who we are by chance or by design?

This is also affirmed in Romans 8:29:

> *"For those God foreknew*
> *he also predestined to become conformed*
> *to the image of His Son,*
> *that he would be the firstborn*
> *among many brothers and sisters."*

We were foreknown to our Father—known and loved even before we were born! We were also equipped to be conformed to the image of Jesus. Sanctification is that process of being conformed to the image of Jesus.

First John 3:1 is another beautiful verse that uplifts us:

"See what great love
the Father has lavished on us,
that we should be called
the children of God."

Most nations, kingdoms, and prestigious societies confer honor on their very distinguished citizens/members by inducting them into the highest echelons of their society and bestowing lofty titles on them. Is there any title that even remotely compares to the one conferred by the God of the Universe on any one of us as "My child," whom He has longed to adopt into His family? He has waited patiently for us to accept and say "yes."

When we acknowledge that honor and undeserved title, we begin to see Him through our inward eye; we hear Him though the scriptures and the promptings of His Spirit and feel Him through our lived experiences. The more we commune with Him, the more familiar we get with Him as our Father and start to discern His nuanced presence and counsel. This gets progressively reaffirmed the more we resonate with His Spirit. Then, we become aware that

"The Spirit Himself
testifies with our spirit
that we are
God's children."

ROMANS 8:16

Communication is a two-way process. We can only imagine God's response to our attempts to reach out to Him.

As an earthly father, I know the joy of hearing from my children (who are now adults and live in another city) when they call individually or when they call together. Decades ago, when they were very young children and could not yet speak articulately, it was still such a thrill to hear their voices or even just their babbling sounds.

I can only imagine that our heavenly Father also exults in our attempts, no matter how feeble, to communicate with Him.

Our Father* in Heaven

* Heavenly humor has it that recent English Bible trans-
lators are no longer patrons of "art in Heaven."

This prayer and all of Jesus's teachings consistently place God, our Father, in Heaven. But, here again, we are dealing with a location we have never been to, nor do we know of anyone else besides Jesus who has made credible claims of having been there (though we may hope/believe that many of our dear ones are there).

"Heaven" is sometimes confused with "the heavens," which refers to the vast expanse of the skies above the earth. The astronomical sciences have developed sophisticated telescopes and devices to search the heavens above and around the earth. Heaven has not been located in the space of "the heavens" for millions of light years around the earth. (One light year equals the distance that light would have traveled at the speed of 186,000 miles per second in one year.)

There is no evidence to support nor refute the speculation that one of the stars (or clusters of stars) may be where Heaven is located.

So where is Heaven? Jesus himself said,

"My kingdom is not of this world."

JOHN 18:36

We are left to consider that Heaven is a metaphysical (beyond the physical realm, as we know it) place or "other-worldly." Heaven, we surmise, is a real place in a different dimension, not in the physical world to which we are accustomed and in which we currently live.

If we accept that our Father is in Heaven, then we can also accept that Heaven is where our Father is. Since Heaven is His Kingdom (the king's domain), our Father is unquestionably sovereign there. As we will see in a few chapters, Heaven is also where the Father's will gets carried out.

So the four characteristics we use in our working concept of Heaven are that

1   Heaven is other-worldly,

2   Heaven is where our Father is,

3   Heaven is where our Father is sovereign, and,

4   Heaven is where His will is carried out without any opposition or resistance.

Earth, by contrast, is physical, where God's presence and sovereignty may not be accepted/acknowledged, and we, its inhabitants, offer resistance to the will of our Father.

But here's some great news. If we acknowledge our Father's presence and His sovereignty, and if we can be totally aligned to His will, we can metaphysically experience Heaven in our minds while here on earth!

Fanny Crosby, the blind hymn writer, is reported to have written more than eight thousand hymns. In 1873, she wrote "Blessed Assurance,"[5] which is still a classic today. In it she expressed the "foretaste of glory divine." One of the joys of praying is that we get to experience that foretaste of divine glory every time we commune with our Father in Heaven.

Since Heaven is our *Father's* home, it is also *our* eventual home. A home where we haven't yet been but look forward to residing in with excitement. We have all experienced the thrill of anticipation when we consider going somewhere exceptionally nice where we haven't been before.

We are told that

> *"What no eye has seen, what no ear has heard,*
> *what no human mind has conceived" —*
> *the things that God has prepared*
> *for those who love Him.*

1 CORINTHIANS 2:9

In other words, what awaits us is something so wonder-filled that it is beyond the limits of our human imagination.

The Psalmist wrote of such ecstasy in Psalm 139:6:

"Such knowledge is too wonderful for me,
too great for me to understand."

Once we accept adoption into God's family through Jesus Christ, we are assured of eternal life with him in his (and our) Father's Kingdom. Therefore, no matter what difficult circumstances we face here on earth, we know that it will be temporary. A permanent home in our Father's Kingdom awaits us. Henceforth, we have citizenship there! The long-lasting ecstasy of that anticipated kingdom (Heaven) can enable us to endure whatever short-term agony we may experience here on earth, perhaps, like a mother enduring excruciating labor pains. Or like Stephen, one of the first martyrs, while he was being stoned to death (see Acts 7:54–60).

Therefore, from now on, we can view where we now live on earth as our temporary lodging and our Father's home, Heaven, as our eventual and permanent home. When it is time, our Father will take us home. Until then, let us do what He has us here to get done.

——— ◆◇◆ ———

My mother had been in an Alive Hospice facility in Nashville for a few days before she died ten years ago. It was an emotionally difficult time for us. But I was greatly comforted by the chaplain there, who described their facility as a *soul nursery*, where the soul is delivered from the physical body and birthed into the eternal, loving presence of our Lord.

——— ◆◇◆ ———

A few years ago, the fast-food chain McDonald's had an interesting advertisement. In it, they showed a toddler on a swing set. When the child would reach the height of the upward arc of the swing, he would break into a smile, only to lose the smile and begin to cry on the downward swing. After a few repetitions of this, they showed the reason for the child's smile. At the height of the swing, the child was able to see, through an open window, McDonald's golden arches that seemed nearby. On the downswing, the child lost sight of McDonald's logo, as a result of which, the smile was replaced with a disappointed cry.[6]

Similarly, as we begin to pray, we get metaphysical glimpses of our Father in His Kingdom of Heaven, and we break into a spiritual smile!

Included when we say *our Father* is also *my Father* for each of us who has accepted adoption into His family. The enormity of that statement could and should leave us awestruck. The God who created and runs the universe and can do absolutely anything and everything is *my* Father! We cannot fully comprehend that with our tender, limited minds.

Little children are known to simply accept that which maybe too complex for them to understand. Can we also, like children, accept our Father and His Kingdom as being beyond our full comprehension, but oh so very dear to us? Jesus himself declared,

"Truly I tell you,
unless you change
and become like little children,
you will never enter
the kingdom of heaven."

MATTHEW 18:3

So now, no matter how humble our circumstances, how undeserving of coming into His presence we may be, by the amazing grace of our Lord Jesus, we have individually been offered adoption by the King of Heaven. When we accept that offer, each of us is transformed into a prince or princess of the Kingdom of Heaven! It is no surprise then, that we enter His courts with praise, exclaiming:

Our Father in Heaven,
hallowed be your name.

CHAPTER 2

HALLOWED BE YOUR NAME

I t is always fitting and appropriate to begin prayer by honoring our Father. "Hallowed" is a word that is not often
used, other than in this prayer. (Even very knowledgeable
contestants in the popular game show *Jeopardy!* couldn't recall
that word in 2023.)[7] It means "greatly revered," "kept holy,"
or "consecrated." After the salutation to God the Father, the
first words of this prayer are "Hallowed be your name." So it
must have significance.

What is a name? A name is a distinctive representation, a
symbol that stands for a specific identity. Because names are
sometimes replicated (think "John Smith"), we often qualify
names by adding a source or origin, for example, Joseph of
Arimathea, or Simon, son of Jonah. But even with those qualifications, there may be more than one with the same name
over the course of time. As a result, we not only have first and
last names, we add middle names too. And sometimes, several of them. And prefixes, suffixes, and titles too. All these
names are to distinguish a particular one from all the others
so that people will know who exactly is being referred to by
that specific name.

When it comes to the name of God, our Father, He was
never named because there was no one else like Him, nor was
there anyone else besides Him to name Him. There is not and
has not been any other God! He had/has no peers.

It is only mankind, His creation, that sought a name by
which to refer to Him (and fights, sometimes to death, over
who has the right name). In response to Moses's question,
"Who shall I say sent me?" God referred to Himself as

"J-H-W-H."

That is translated as "I AM WHO I AM" or "The Self-Existing One."

There are millions of dads in the world. But when we call out "Dad," "Daddy," "Papa," or any equivalent, we know exactly who we mean, and so does he. Similarly, when we say "Our Father," we know exactly who we mean, and so does He.

How, then, does His name get hallowed? "Hallowed be your name" is an appropriate veneration and glorification of our Father. But, at the start of the prayer, it is worth reminding ourselves of an essential aspect in all prayer. Prayer is **not** about instructing God what to do (even if it is done very politely)!

Often, for the most part, our prayers sound like a set of chores we leave for God to have addressed before we return with our next round of requests or instructions for Him. Let us always be reverent and mindful of who is God and who is the supplicant. Delegating to God would make Him our subordinate! So whenever we ask for God's help with something, it is wise to ensure that we have done all that we can do about it ourselves and are humbly asking for His help because we cannot accomplish it ourselves.

Remember, when we say "Hallowed be your name," we are not asking God to somehow orchestrate the hallowing of His own name. It is a reminder to us that we need to do all we can to hallow *His* name.

One of the great utterances in the Bible, Psalm 118:26, echoed during the celebrations as Jesus entered Jerusalem a week before he was crucified was

"Blessed is he who comes in the name of the Lord."

As disciples (or *wannabe* disciples), we accept, without hesitation, that Jesus came in the name of the Lord. But now that we have been adopted into God the Father's family, it dawns on us that *we* also have His name.

"God decided in advance to adopt us into His own family by bringing us to himself through Jesus Christ."

EPHESIANS 1:5

NEW LIVING TRANSLATION

Yes, we have been adopted by Him. It is as though we have an added last name now that we are sons and daughters of the Most High. We bear His name! Wherever we go, we too go in the name of the Lord, though we usually think we are *incognito*. We may dismiss having His name as too lofty, that we are clearly undeserving of calling it our own. But it is a choice we have to make. Do we accept or reject the offer to be adopted into His family? If we accept, it is appropriate for us to repeatedly reflect that "I am now the son or daughter of the Lord God of the universe."

What a privilege! But with privilege comes responsibility. We belong to the Royal Priesthood. As the apostle Peter wrote,

"But you are a chosen people, a royal priesthood, a holy nation, God's special possession, that you may declare the praises of him who called you out of darkness into his wonderful light."

1 PETER 2:9 NIV

Let us never let the awe fade of being adopted into the family of the Creator of the universe (or multiverse) through the sacrificial love and grace of our Lord Jesus! We will address this further in subsequent chapters.

Please note that we have all been called out of darkness. It is worth recognizing that we didn't get selected because any of us were exceptional, or superior, or deserving. It is simply by grace. Undeserved favor. *Sola gratia!*

We are called upon to *declare the praises* of Him who called us. That's one of the ways we hallow His name. Let us also reflect on what happens to us when we accept Jesus's invitation to be adopted into his Father's family and bear His name. The apostle Paul says

"For all of you who were baptized into Christ
have clothed yourselves with Christ."

GALATIANS 3:27

It is interesting to consider that a requirement of all entrants into the Kingdom of Heaven is to be clothed "with Christ." It is as though we have been given a garment to put over ourselves that identifies us as belonging to Jesus Christ. Acceptance of Jesus's invitation to his Father's Kingdom is "salvation." Salvation changes our identity and our destiny. Our old selves, in our previous identities, would not be acceptable in the Kingdom of Heaven. But this new garment which we spiritually don identifies us as "with Christ,"; hence, we are now acceptable in the Kingdom with this new identity. Henceforth, we are to be identified as being "with Christ" and a member of the Father's household.

Our destiny has also changed. We are saved from perdition (our former destiny to perish when our season is done on earth) and are earmarked for eternity with Jesus. We are set on the way to the Father's Kingdom. The Jesus way—the only way there.

"Therefore, if anyone is in Christ, he is a new creation.
The old has passed away; behold, the new has come."

2 CORINTHIANS 5:17
ENGLISH STANDARD VERSION

The old is behind us. The new beckons to us. Jesus is the *template* for our new selves. Our salvation now leads to sanctification, which is the process of progressive transformation to be more Christ-like. And this prayer, as we shall see, leads us through sanctification.

Before "commoners" marry into royal families, they are schooled in etiquette and protocols so that their conduct and attire may befit and be consistent with that of a royal. There is no such requirement *before* we join the most royal family by far. But, once we join this family, we have a constant, ever-present tutor, a helper and counselor, the Holy Spirit, who guides us in the ways of the new life. He spiritually grooms (sanctifies) us to be more and more Christ-like.

You may have come across communications which are signed off with the phrase "In Him" or "In Christ." The writers in these instances are professing to be representing service to God, to Jesus Christ, or claiming to be in His extended family. If we have reason to question their "Christ-likeness," we would regard their communication with skepticism. We must bear in mind that all our utterances, actions, and communications are effectively being signed off "In Him" even when we don't add that byline. Once adopted by Him, we become His ambassadors and always represent Him. Always! When we do so appropriately and also when we misrepresent Him. It is through our thoughts, words, and deeds that we hallow—or fail to hallow—His name!

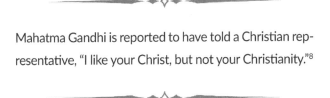

Mahatma Gandhi is reported to have told a Christian representative, "I like your Christ, but not your Christianity."[8]

Once accepted into our Father's family, our *choice* is not taken away. We still have the choice to live "in Christ" or "in our way." Our ability to choose what we do is probably our most treasured privilege. It is also man's greatest stumbling block, simply because of the number of unwise and dangerous options available to us. We will address this in greater detail in subsequent chapters. This prayer makes us mindful of our tendency to live in our own way, and reminds us to seek the Holy Spirit's help to live "in Christ."

A verse of the song by Adelaide Pollard (sung so beautifully by Jim Reeves) comes to mind:

> *Have Thine own way, Lord*
>
> *Have Thine own way*
>
> *Hold over my being absolute sway*
>
> *Filled with Thy Spirit till all can see*
>
> *Christ only always, living in me.*[9]

Are we such followers of Christ that others see glimpses of Christ when they encounter us?

One of the most haunting verses in the Bible is in the Gospel of Luke. After the last supper with his disciples, on the eve of his crucifixion, Jesus led them to the garden of Gethsemane. Judas arrived there with a crowd of guards and soldiers. He then stepped forward to kiss Jesus in order to identify him.

Jesus asked him,

> *"Judas, are you betraying*
> *the Son of Man with a kiss?"*

LUKE 22:48

It is a question worth asking ourselves. Do we profess to be His when it suits us, claiming familiarity and our kinship with Him, but conduct ourselves in ways inconsistent with or opposed to His ways? Could Jesus ask that question of us:

"_____, are you betraying the Son of Man with a kiss?"

Do our daily lives honor Him and, in so doing, hallow His name? Or do we betray Him and align ourselves with desires and actions that distance us from Him?

Do we intensely seek the side of our Lord and feed on what He imparts to us? Or do we subscribe to an opposing worldview that aligns us with those who undermine His ways and teachings? We are reminded that

"Blessed is the one
who does not walk in step with the wicked
or stand in the way that sinners take
or sit in the company of mockers."

PSALM 1:1

Wickedness is not so much the morbidity of one's actions as it is the motivating desires that drive our actions — the *mens rea* underlying our *actus reus* (more of that in chapter 6).

A searing, oft quoted question, whose original authorship I have not yet been able to determine, asks: "If you were arrested for being a follower of Christ, would there be enough evidence to convict you?" The question is not really whether *people* think you are a follower of Christ but what God, our Father, would say. Does our life honor and hallow His name or betray it?

As we will see in the next chapter, we are urged to seek to emulate life in Heaven. We are told in Revelation 4:8 that in heaven, the living creatures around the throne never stop saying

"Holy, holy, holy, (hallowed)
is the Lord God Almighty,
who was, and is, and is come."

(PARENTHESIS MINE)

As we in our spirit enter the throne room of our Father, let us also seek to always hallow His name.

If you feel convicted of having betrayed Him, like I have (oh so many countless times), please do not despair nor hide away from Him. For we know that

"If we confess our sins,
He is faithful and just and
will forgive us our sins
and purify us
from all unrighteousness."

1 JOHN 1:9

That forgiveness and purification is available and necessary for all of us. It is essential for our sanctification. Obviously, none of us can change the past. All we can do is to seek and receive the forgiveness and cleansing by the mercy and grace of our Lord Jesus. Having done so, let us undertake, by the counsel of the Holy Spirit, to always reverence and exalt His name through all facets of our lives henceforth.

Jesus also taught his disciples of an indirect way to hallow the Father's name.

"Let your light shine before others,
that they may see your good deeds

and glorify your Father in Heaven."

MATTHEW 5:16

Jesus declared that he was the light of the world (John 8:12). Jesus also exhorted his disciples to be (reflected) lights to the world. By what we do, guided by the Holy Spirit and reflecting what Jesus would have done (WWJD—see chapter 4), our deeds can lead to others hallowing the name of the Father.

So, both directly and indirectly, in all we do in thought, word, and deed, at all times, hallowed be His name.

RECAP

Thus far, this prayer has made us aware of Jesus having offered us adoption into his Father's family and kingdom. When we accept this offer, no matter what our past has been, we are exalted and transformed into princes and princesses in the Kingdom of Heaven. Jesus Father has become our Father too. We have a new identity and a new citizenship! The old self is behind us, forgiven. A future in a new identity, *child of God*, beckons to us. Citizenship in Heaven has been conferred on us. We have become part of the privileged "Body of Christ." Heaven is our Father's home and, therefore, our eventual home too. Our stay on earth is a temporary posting. We get glimpses of Heaven whenever we are aware of the presence of God, acknowledge His sovereignty, and submit totally to His will.

As a result of our adoption and transformation, we acknowledge our former errant ways, and seek and accept forgiveness and cleansing. Having done so, we revere His name, recognizing that it is now our name too. We have received salvation and commenced the process of sanctification. It is henceforth both our honor and responsibility to hallow His name, directly and indirectly, serving as His ambassadors at *all* times.

CHAPTER 3

YOUR KINGDOM COME

In the Introduction, we already emphasized that prayer was essentially about alignment with God. Matthew 6:10 directs us to that alignment more than any other verse in the Bible. It is the crux of this prayer and provides the directional compass to reorient our lives. Let's begin by addressing the first part of this verse:

Your Kingdom come.

Unlike a thousand years ago, most of us don't live in recognized kingdoms today, though some kingdoms are still present, e.g., the United Kingdom, Kingdom of Saudi Arabia, etc. We think of kingdoms as lands or geographic territories ruled by a king, queen or sultan. But, of course, it isn't really the land that is ruled. Nor is it the flora or fauna of the land. It is the people of a land, who acknowledge a monarch, to whose rule they subject themselves, that make it a kingdom. People and nations outside that kingdom may also accord recognition to the kingdom and its monarch. But those people and nations typically do not grant the monarch any authority over them. Please note this because it has significant bearing in the context of our faith.

When we say "Your kingdom come," it may be comforting for us to believe that we would welcome God establishing His Kingdom on earth. And, of course, we would be thrilled to live in that Kingdom. Here again, we are at risk of asking God to *do the work* of establishing His Kingdom on earth. We stand ready to proffer our approval and acceptance if and when He does so!

We may also subscribe, with confidence, to the view that His Kingdom will come at some point in time and offer token support for that notion. However, we tend to be passive observers waiting for that event to unfold. We may even affirm that if it were to occur during our lifetime, we will be found among the applauding throng, along the lines of the crowd shouting, "Hosanna" as Jesus rode into Jerusalem, less than a week before the same crowd perhaps stood by, watching his crucifixion.

The truth is that He has already established His Kingdom! Yes, here on earth. The crucial question, though, is: Do we belong to His Kingdom? Are we His subjects? Or are we outsiders speculating about His Kingdom, refusing to grant Him decisive authority over us?

Jesus warned his listeners that many think they belong to His Kingdom but do not!

"Not everyone who says to me 'Lord, Lord,' will enter the kingdom of heaven, but only the one who does the will of my Father who is in heaven."

MATTHEW 7:21

Our Father's Kingdom is where He is sovereign. We may mollify ourselves saying that we do recognize Him as sovereign. But do we recognize Him as *a* sovereign or as *my* sovereign? If we just recognize Him as a sovereign, we are like the people who don't belong to His Kingdom but acknowledge that He does have a kingdom. He does not have dominion over us. We are mere onlookers with varying degrees of interest in the happenings in His Kingdom.

On the other hand, if He is *my* sovereign, then He has absolute dominion over me. Everything that I have is His, including all my possessions, my relationships, my work, my family, my time, and my plans. Even my life and my will!

Craig Groeschel coined the term "the Christian atheist" to refer to us when we believe in God but live as if He doesn't exist.[10]

As we saw on page 35, the Kingdom of Heaven is where the Father's presence is, where He is sovereign and where His will encounters no resistance. Prayer is always the opportunity to experience His Kingdom while here on earth. That means that we have an opportunity to experience the Father's Kingdom here on earth as it is in Heaven, if we

i.   Acknowledge His presence,

ii. Grant Him absolute sovereignty, and

iii. Submit to His will without any resistance.

And lo! His Kingdom is in us and we are in His Kingdom. Along the lines of Jesus urging his followers to

"Remain in me
as I also remain in you."

JOHN 15:4

The price to experience Heaven is to grant Him absolute sovereignty through our absolute surrender![11]

In Matthew 16:24, Jesus said,

"Whoever wants to be my disciple
must deny themselves
and take their cross and follow Me."

We have heard of (and perhaps even talked of) surrendering our lives to God. We tend to kid ourselves that what that means is a *willingness* to surrender our lives, but not being *really* called upon to surrender unless He appears before us, or we audibly hear Him asking us to surrender, like Saul of Tarsus did.

This reminds me of a satirical account of a church pastor who put all the offerings presented by the congregation on a large bedsheet. He and the church elders then held the corners of the bedsheet and tossed the offerings up in the air (heavenward), inviting God to take any or all of it. All that fell back was then considered granted by God to be used by the pastor as he pleased.

In a wrestling match, if one wrestler finds himself pinned down by the other with no way out, he can tap the mat to indicate submission/surrender, which then permits him to get out of the opponent's grip. But then, he rises up off the mat and gets set for the next round of the match.

Similarly, in a game of chess, when faced with a losing situation, we topple our king over to indicate surrender and acceptance of defeat. But, moments later, we pick it up, rearrange our pieces and get set for the next game! We often think of surrender as a temporary suspension of our freedom to engage in combat, typically with the intention of arraying ourselves again shortly thereafter, for the next round of battle.

But surrender is total submission! When a soldier surrenders on the battlefield, he has to lay down his arms. He does not get to pick up his arms later that day. Or ever, unless his captor decides to release him.

In real life, a decision to surrender our lives requires us to grant God primacy in all our decisions. All of them. Important and unimportant ones. That requires us to frequently and repeatedly align ourselves with God in prayer. Hence the exhortation,

"Pray continually."

I THESSALONIANS 5:17

We can be in a continual state of alignment with God, even if we are not continually conversing with Him in our minds, in prayer.

Surrender is perhaps best depicted symbolically, in baptism. During baptism, we consent to die to ourselves (deny ourselves) when we get immersed. Rising up out of the water represents resurrection into a life (of following Jesus) aligned to the Father, the Son, and the Holy Spirit.

But what are we surrendering? We surrender our individual kingdoms. As ordinary people, do we have kingdoms of our own? Yes, we do. Our individual kingdoms are our spheres of influence. Our selves, our families, our friends, our teams, our work, our possessions, our hopes and dreams, and our interests and priorities. Please note, the greatest impediment that keeps us from seeking the Kingdom of God is . . . our own kingdom!

Our kingdoms are what we worry about. We get so wrapped up in the demands of our own kingdoms that the Kingdom of God gets relegated into the background—something to get to—after we address the pressing needs of our own kingdom. But we have so many items we feel we need to attend to that we never seem to get to a point that we feel we have dealt with them all.

Paraphrasing Dr. Richard Carlson, who pointed out in his book *Don't Sweat the Small Stuff . . . and It's All Small Stuff*, our in-box will never be empty even on the day we die.[12]

In our lives, we feel we have so many obligations to take care of, horizons to explore, or interests to pursue. There always seem to be things we feel we need to do (or want to do) as well as matters concerning others or other events in "our kingdom" that are pressing.

So what was Jesus asking his disciples to do? A little later in the same chapter where this prayer is recorded, we learn that Jesus exhorted his followers to

"Seek first the Kingdom of God . . ."

MATTHEW 6:33

Jesus asks that we change our priorities!

The basic goal of any stage is to make it to the *next* stage. A basic goal for a kindergartener (or for their parents) is for him/her to make it to the first grade. The basic goal when we take off in an airplane is to land at our destination. The basic goal of an elective pregnancy is a live birth. The primary goal of this life, Jesus emphasized, is to make it to the next (eternal) life!

Many people do not subscribe to the belief in a life beyond death. For them, this life is all there is. They do have the right to believe so. But, if so, it would then make sense to try and maximize the subjective sense of gratification and success during this life. That leads to satisfying our many appetites and pursuing our passions, including those that may laudably advance the common good or even those that could eventually harm us or others. Some might rationalize doing harm if, in the process, subjective gratification is enhanced. After all, most of the harm in this world occurs as a byproduct of some persons, communities, or nations seeking their own advantage! Hedonism and exploitation become understandable. As does even a psychopathic lifestyle. In this system, there could be (seeming) winners and losers. But the common denominator for all such lives, lived in conformity to this system, is that at their end, they perish.

Now the good news for everyone in the system that Jesus proclaimed was (is) that everyone could be winners . . . even Lazarus, who lay covered in sores, begging at the rich man's gate! (See Luke 16:19–28.) Jesus offered the option of life beyond death here on earth, in the Kingdom of His Father. And Jesus made that Kingdom accessible to *anybody* who so wished. Jesus said

"For God so loved the world,

that He gave His only begotten Son,

that whosoever believes in him (Jesus)*

shall not perish but have eternal life."

JOHN 3:16 ESV

* PARENTHESIS MINE

Perishing at the end of our earthly lives is like a pregnancy ending in a stillbirth. Utterly tragic!

I recall a powerful sermon by our former pastor Doug Fultz at Franklin Christian Church in Tennessee. He presented a presumed conversation between twins in the womb, just before their time of delivery.

Paraphrasing Pastor Doug, one twin says to the other, "Our life in this world is coming to an end; it was fun for a long time, but it has become very cramped and uncomfortable here. I dread what lies ahead; I fear there will be too much pain."

The other replies, "No, I am confident there is life beyond this world that we have known. I have felt the love of a parent and have had sensations of a world beyond what we have known here."

The first one retorts, "What unfounded beliefs! Has anybody been to the life you talk about beyond this world?"

The other again responds, "You are right that we haven't been there, nor do we know anyone who has been to the world beyond ours. But I feel certain that there is a whole different world beyond this. I am sure the love of my parent will receive me into whatever that world turns out to be."

Annoyed, the first one shouts, "You and your baseless feelings! Then why don't you go find that world and leave me some more space here?"

To which the other replies, "Peace, brother, I am not afraid. I will willingly go ahead of you. I so wish that you, too, will be there with me in the world that awaits us."

The overarching outcome needed of life in our earthly kingdom, regardless of our experiences during its duration, is to make it to the life in the Kingdom of God. Getting to the Kingdom of God is our top priority. Or we will end up perishing . . . needlessly.

If we were to write down our priorities in order of significance and commitment, Priority #1 matters more than Priority #2, which, in turn, matters more than Priority #3, and so forth. We often think of accomplishing all our identified priorities. But, in reality, we almost never do. If we are pushed to make a choice, we might need to give up a lower-order priority in order to accomplish a higher one. Extending that further, we might need to give up Priority #3 to accomplish Priority #2. Taken one step further still, we might even need to give up Priority #2, if that was the price to pay, to accomplish Priority #1. It could therefore be worth giving up everything relating to our earthly kingdom, if necessary, to gain the Kingdom of God, if Priority #1 was the Kingdom of God.

Man cannot earn his way to the Kingdom of God the Father. Nor can any striving, however heroic, accomplish that goal. It is a gift offered by the Father, relayed by Jesus, to any and all who believe.

I love the word "whosoever" in John 3:16, quoted above. No earthly qualifications required. No accomplishments needed. No religiosity or piety. Not even any good deeds. No disqualifications either. Nothing, no matter how awful, disqualifies us. Merely believe and accept Jesus's offer. He will do the rest. But we need to stay totally surrendered.

The Kingdom of God has already come, in some measure. It will come into its full extent with or without any particular one of us. None of us are individually essential to the Kingdom of God. But out of God's amazing love for us, He invites us into His Kingdom while we are yet undeserving of that invitation. Because He sees us not for who we are but for who we can be in Jesus.

"But God showed His great love for us in that while we were still sinners, Christ died for us."

ROMANS 5:8

Undeserving though we are, the joy of the being in Kingdom of Heaven with Jesus beckons to us. Is there anything more valuable to us that we would choose to spurn that invitation and prefer to perish? Some regrettably do.

That prompted C S Lewis, in his book *The Great Divorce*, to write, "All that are in Hell choose it." [13] The only ones who end up not in Heaven are the ones who reject the offer and, possibly, those unaware of that offer (though there are interpretations of verses in the Bible that the offer may be made to them later).

This is also the opportune time in our prayer to present our own kingdoms to the Lord: our particular challenges, our dear ones and their challenges, health, finances, jobs, uncertainties, hopes and fears, and the ones for whom we wish to intercede.

When we surrender our kingdom to the Father, it and all its problems become His. We ask Him to please manage them as part of His Kingdom. It is certainly appropriate for us to bring our problems to the Lord for Him to determine the solution. The trap we usually fall into is that we often think we know the best solution to our problems. We have to guard against asking God to do our bidding by giving us the solution of *our* choice.

Our own kingdoms usually are our priority even during the times we pray. We often seek divine favor to prosper our own kingdoms and the kingdoms of those dear to us. Because we are so concerned about the ramifications of our kingdoms, we may not get around to considering God's Kingdom and His will. We worry that our kingdom may suffer if we aren't its principal caretakers. Please note that any kingdom other than His Kingdom is a rival kingdom. That makes our kingdom a *rival kingdom*. We must decide whether we pursue His Kingdom or our own rival kingdom.

One vital consideration before we move on: No matter how vexed the state of our lives or of those who matter dearly to us in our kingdoms, a pivotal question begs an answer.

Who could manage our problematic situations better? We or God? We will address this further in the following chapter.

If and when we surrender *all* of our kingdom to Him to be part of His Kingdom, then we can truly say "Your kingdom come," and we can be assured that our kingdom will be cared for, better than if we did so by ourselves.

"Your kingdom come" also refers to the anticipated millennial reign of Jesus, when he comes again (see Revelation

20:2–3). Believers look forward to the return of Jesus in glory and, per the Bible, will even reign with him. Followers of Jesus in the first century are reported to have used the Aramaic word *Maranatha*[14] as an expressed hope of his second coming, when parting. That is translated as "Lord, come" when it is broken down as marana-tha. Interestingly, when that word is broken down as maran-atha, it translates as "Lord has come." With either translation, maranatha appropriately invokes our Lord, who was and is, and is to come (see Revelation 4:8).

The apostle Paul also used the word maranatha at the end of his letter to the Corinthians[15] (see 1 Corinthians 16:22). Additionally, that is a term used in the *Didache*, a second-century document of patristic literature considered to include the teachings of the disciples.[16]

More relevant than the world around us is the world within us in our minds. Is that world part of His Kingdom? If it is, then, we must be prepared for His will to be done in us—and, through us—here on earth as it is in Heaven. Because His Kingdom and His will are inseparable.

CHAPTER 4

YOUR WILL BE DONE ON EARTH AS IT IS IN HEAVEN

This verse at its outset acknowledges that God's will is not routinely done on earth, though it is in Heaven. Genesis 1:27 says that God created man in His own image. Not in His physical image but with God's nature and will imprinted in him. God also created man with the ability and freedom to make choices. Otherwise, man would be robotic. Presented with a wide array of options, could man arrive at the right choice other than through trial and error? Could and would man recognize his errors when he chose wrongly? Statistically, we would run out of life long before we exhausted even a tiny fraction of the available options.

Over time, the imprinted will of God in man has been overgrown with choice patterns learned from each person's own lived experiences and from those around them. One of the powerful effects of the relatively recent phenomenon of globalization in human history, along with advances in technology, is that man is not just influenced by the persons in his own family or neighborhood; he is now influenced by fads even from distant corners of the world. Beset with so many options, at so many crossroads of life, is there a way for man to make the right choices? Consistently? Comparatively, finding the proverbial needle in a haystack would seem a much easier task.

The mind of a young child is presented with a bewildering amount of informational inputs and choices. The child is usually guided by parents or other family members in making choices early in their lives. As the children grow, they assess for themselves whether the recommendations of their elders are appropriate for them and whether those recommendations worked well for the parents. If so, choice patterns get established.

Once choice patterns are established in childhood, there is a likelihood that they will persist into adulthood (see Proverbs 22:6). But an impactful change in environment and informational inputs (like when a youth leaves home) can lead to a disruption of established behavioral patterns and the eventual development of new ones, sometimes very different from the previous ones.

We all go through a psychological process of "separation-individuation," (usually from infancy through adolescence) in which we recognize ourselves as separate from our parent(s) and develop our own individual identities (and choices) which we see as distinct from those of our parents or their surrogates.

The most vital of choices for us (very often, unrecognized) is whether or not to abide by our understood and imprinted will of God. Many disregard any role that God might play in the choices they make and instead operate on the principle of expediency. Decisions and choices tend to be made heuristically (using mental shortcuts which are sometimes inaccurate).

The Bible does not explicitly state what led to Satan's fall from Heaven. One of the conjectures is that Satan dissented regarding man being granted free will. He may well have predicted that man would make a series of choices that drew him further and further away from the will of God, thereby rendering man an unsatisfactory creation, if yielding to God's will was central to his design.

God, though, would have foreseen that having created man with the ability to make choices and exercise free will, they would all pursue errant options. But God had made man knowing that at least some of them, who avail of their access to forgiveness, would steer their will back to their understood will of God.

Perhaps, Satan arrogantly maintained that he could prove God wrong by demonstrating that man would never surrender that will back to God. Much of what is attributed to Satan are efforts to lead man astray and away from God and His will.

Satan's imputed contention is proved right each time man knowingly chooses his own desires over what he believes the will of God to be. Or when man does not even consider what God's will might be. But, God, like the father in the story of the prodigal son (see Luke 15:11–32), waits patiently and confidently for His child to return and submit to the father again.

Satan was emphatically proved wrong by Jesus submitting to the will of the Father, completing a life lived entirely in accordance with the will of the Father ... even to the point of death on the cross.

Jesus, on the night before he faced an excruciating death, cried out,

"Father, if you are willing, take this cup from me,
yet not my will, but Yours be done."

LUKE 22:42

That was perfect submission! Satan's contention was destroyed. Jesus had endured and triumphed to the very end. He could truly and justifiably say,

"It is finished."

JOHN 19:30

We hear echoes of that submission elsewhere too.

As a young maiden, the blessed Mary, mother of Jesus, responded to the angel who startled her with news (never before heard, although prophesied by Isaiah) that she, a virgin, would bear a child by the Holy Spirit while she was already betrothed to Joseph with

> *"Behold the handmaid of the Lord;*
> *be it unto me according to your word."*

LUKE 1:38

KING JAMES VERSION

Abraham, at age 75, responded to God's call to leave his family and the place he had lived in to go to an unknown land that God would show him (see Genesis 12: 1–4).

Abraham trusted God's promise that He would provide Abraham a son, even though he and his wife were way past the childbearing age (see Genesis 15:1–6).

Abraham was even willing to offer Isaac, that miraculously born son, as a sacrifice when God asked him to do so (see Genesis 22:1–8).

Moses, despite severe misgivings (he had fled the country after killing an Egyptian), agreed to return to Pharaoh's court in Egypt with a preposterous demand that Pharaoh let all the Israelite slaves go out of the country to worship God, because God had asked him to. (see Exodus 3:1–4:18).

Shadrach, Meshach, and Abednego, even at the risk of being thrown into the fiery furnace, refused to worship the image of King Nebuchadnezzar. They were saved by God after being thrown into the furnace (see Daniel 3:12–28).

Daniel refused to stop praying to God, despite the threat of being thrown into a lion's den. He was protected by God in the lion's den (see Daniel 6:7–23).

Let us not forget countless missionaries and martyrs, through the millennia and even today, who have labored in and for the Kingdom of God, even at the cost of their lives.

The gospel, the exceedingly good news, is that each one of us has the opportunity to make it to the next stage—the Kingdom of God. But in the Kingdom of God, there is no room for anything but the will of God. The requirement for those drawn to His Kingdom, therefore, is that we yield to God's will. It bears repetition that God's Kingdom and His will are inseparable. The second part of Jesus's cautionary verse highlights this:

"Not everyone who says to me
'Lord, Lord' will enter into the kingdom of heaven,
but only the one who does the will
of my Father who is in heaven."

MATTHEW 7:21

God's will often seems very nebulous to us. Lives that seem to be consistently lived according to His will are not often modeled before us. God does not appear physically (nor in apparitions) to most of us. Since He doesn't seem to give us instructions from day to day about what He wants us to do, we tend to do the best we can, using our own judgment. After all, that's what almost everybody else seems to be doing. As a result, we may stumble through life, doing what appeals to us or, what others seem to be doing and risk failing to reach His Kingdom. We may attribute that to not having clear enough directions and because most others seem to be on similar paths. If it seems good enough for our families and friends, we conclude that it's probably good enough for us. Human decisions are greatly influenced by the decisions of their peers.

We all have the ability and propensity to project our lives and circumstances into an imagined future, both immediate and distant. Dissatisfactions with those projections can lead to anxiety, depression, anger, and desperation. Our behavioral choices tend to be goal directed or habitual. We make choices to try and alter our projected futures, or we continue in maintenance patterns that have been established by repetition. We also tend to cluster with those who perceive our environment like we do. In the process, we are influenced by them and respond to our environment like they do. That contributes to our herd behavior.

But Jesus himself warned his listeners in Matthew 7:13–14:

> *"Wide is the gate and broad is the road*
> *that leads to destruction,*
> *and many enter through it.*
> *But small is the gate and narrow the road*
> *that leads to life,*
> *and only a few find it."*

So how can we find the small gate and narrow road of His will in our daily lives? We need to be guided by His will rather than by society. Upon probing deeper, we find that God had revealed His will through the scriptures, even in Old Testament times.

> *"And what does the Lord require of you? To act justly and*
> *to love mercy and to walk humbly with your God."*

MICAH 6:8

The call to act justly requires us to go beyond merely not engaging in anything that is blatantly unjust. We have to ensure justice for our neighbors, who may be denied it, overlooked by us or even by others. We do become our neighbor's keepers. The deeper question is "Who is our neighbor?" and how far our community extends. That was the question that led to Jesus's parable of the good samaritan (see Luke 10:25–37).

This also ties in another salutary exhortation from King Solomon:

"Do not withhold good from those to whom it is due,

when it is in your power to act."

PROVERBS 3:27

How eager are we to effect good when we can? Are we willing for others to benefit from what we do, even more than we? We are urged to love our neighbor as ourselves. Is our neighbor's kingdom as dear to us as our own kingdom? Can we accept everyone we come across as our neighbor? We can, if we see everyone as potential members of His Kingdom, which would make all of us one famil—children of the same Father!

But we often have a problem with that. A judgmental one. The people around us (including us) are so deeply flawed that they (and we) don't seem eligible for the Kingdom of Heaven.

The solution to that quandary is mercy. Mercy looks beyond the flaws; nay, it cleanses the flaws, because the penalty for the flaws has already been paid by the death of Jesus on the cross (as addressed in chapter 6). I can accept that His mercy cleanses me. But, if it does, it must necessarily be able to cleanse all others too, because I am as undeserving of His mercy as anyone else. Thankfully, there's plenty of mercy made available. As the Psalmist says,

"For, you Lord, are good,

and ready to forgive,

and abundant in mercy

to all those who call upon you."

PSALM 86:5 (NKJV)

"The Lord is merciful
and gracious,
slow to anger and
abounding in mercy."

PSALM 103:8 (KJV)

When we love mercy, it prompts us to trade our judgmental glasses for compassionate ones. It changes our view of the world and of our fellow men.

And, of course, walking humbly with the Lord is the essence of prayer. How else can we walk with the one who showed us mercy and grace by dying for us? It is His mercy that gives us the courage to walk with Him when our instinct is to run and hide in shame (see Genesis 3:10). Walking humbly is also the hallmark of the disciple. Jesus's statement to his disciples when he called them was simply, "Follow me" (Matt. 4:19 NIV).

Additionally, by way of instruction, Jesus said,

"A new commandment I give you:
Love one another. As I have loved you,
so you must love one another."

JOHN 13:34

Love is clearly the key! But what *kind* of love?

Love is the affinity, the desire to be with, that seeks the best for the one who is loved. Human love is egocentric (self-oriented), desirous, appetitive, possessive, and consumptive. Divine love is allocentric (oriented towards others), altruistic, benevolent, and self-expending.

Human nature leads us to be attracted to that which appeals to our senses as lovable or to that/those we consider *our own*. Many of those we encounter, especially the needy and those different from us, may not quite seem to make the "lovable" grade. But God invites us into His family, which therefore renders everybody who is potentially a member of His (and, therefore, our) family, our *own*.

Additionally, God has a particularly consistent constituency, beloved to Him, of whom we need to take note. His constituency consists of the needy, the poor, the widow, the orphan, the foreigner: the have-nots! (See Deuteronomy 15:11; Isaiah 1: 17; Proverbs 14:31, 31:8 –9; Jeremiah 22:3; Zechariah 7:10; and 1 John 3:17.) Please read these passages and heed the instructions.

Parents, of course, delight in their accomplished children. But it is the children who struggle and are not thriving who are foremost in the hearts and minds of the parents. So it is with God. And He reaches out to those children in need through those who do His will. His willing followers serve as His hands and feet. Dare we ignore or look down on the ones dearest to God?

Human perception often feeds a judgmental attitude. We tend to blame the needy for their plight and may conclude that their choices and actions landed them where they find themselves. We are so often like the older brother in the parable of the prodigal son (see Luke 15:25–32). It allows us feel absolved from any responsibility towards the disenfranchised. But Jesus himself proclaimed,

"Whatever you did for one of the least
of these brothers and sisters of mine,
you did for me."

MATTHEW 25:40

*"By this everyone will know
that you are my disciples,
if you love one another."*

It takes divine love to break through barriers and see everyone created in His image as our own kin to whom we are then drawn to extend a helping hand.

Most of us have grown up valuing the independence of our minds. We make our own choices from the many options we have. We consider ourselves autonomous. We prize our freedom. After all, the choices we make are what make us who we are. Giving that up, we fear, will require us to give up who we are!

At baseline, instead of seeking to discern God's will, we are prone to be more influenced by people around us (physically or virtually) who seem similar to us. Blending in and being like others can give us a sense of comfort and allay our anxiety.

John Maynard Keynes proposed the herding theory, which addressed the motivations to imitate and follow the crowd in response to uncertainty and perceptions of their own ignorance.[17] Though Keynes primarily addressed patterns relating to financial investing and economics, the herding theory generalizes into common human behavior and how choices are made, especially in settings of uncertainty.

Against that backdrop, the apostle Paul urges us to

*"Be transformed
by the renewing of your mind."*

ROMANS 12:2

But how do we do that?

Some of us, depending on our age, likely grew up before the widespread use of the Global Positioning System (GPS).[18] When we were later introduced to the advantages of GPS, it enabled us to embark on journeys that we may not have otherwise attempted. GPS uses satellites to pinpoint our location, wherever we are, as well as our chosen destination, wherever that may be, and guides us along the best route to get there. Even if we don't follow the recommended directions and choose a different route that gets us lost, GPS will recalibrate and come up with the optimal recommendation to get to our destination from wherever we find ourselves. Even more sophisticated than surface navigation is air and space navigation, which has to contend with three dimensions, other moving aircraft, or celestial bodies, while the earth itself is moving.

Similarly, the transformation of our minds involves tuning in through prayer to the Spiritual Positioning System (SPS). SPS is figuratively employed by the all-knowing Holy Spirit, who identifies the state of our soul, whatever that state may be, and guides us to the Kingdom of our Father by the *way* established by Jesus. When we get lost by pursuing our own impetuous whims, our SPS simply recalibrates and redirects us; that is, if we are willing to accept redirection. A great risk that we face lies in becoming complacent. We may think that we can manage by ourselves and get to our destinations without the assistance of this SPS. We may be too stubborn and lack the humility to seek assistance. Most of those who don't enjoy the benefits of SPS are sadly unaware that it is available to them.

Servomechanisms came into general utilization in the second half of the nineteenth century. Servomechanisms are feedback loops that provide inputs that result in the alteration, as necessary, of the direction, rate, or power of a mechanized system.[19]

Our SPS is a spiritual feedback loop, operated by the Holy Spirit, that facilitates the correction of our spiritual position and the decisions that flow from it. The Holy Spirit lets us know when we get off track, if we are sensitive to that feedback. That spiritual reorientation effects the transformation and renewing of our minds. The Holy Spirit, being God Himself, of course knows the will of God. He steers us into alignment with His will, if only we are willing to be steered. We all need frequent renewal and resets.

Prayer is more than touching base with God once in a while or even regularly every day. It is the repeated fine tuning, seeking alignment with His Spirit. It is a continual SPS for our soul and our will. If, as the earlier part of this verse (Matthew 6:10) says, we are committed to His Kingdom being established in our lives and our kingdoms, we must stand ready to enact His will. And prayer provides the avenue to seek His will. It enables us to be transformed by realigning our minds and our will to His.

We know that we have all fallen short and have failed to abide by God's will. When our lives are in disorder, disharmony, and strife, we may feel powerless to change it ourselves. Yet there is hope. If we yield to His will, transformation is possible. Let's revisit 1 John 1:9, that says,

"If we confess our sins,
He is faithful and just
and will forgive us our sins
and purify us from
all unrighteousness."

This forgiveness available to us countless times. Each time we are purified, we experience a reset. Our spiritual positioning system gets us realigned to His will. We are then provided the opportunity, starting afresh, to simply follow Him.

Jesus directed us toward the goal of seeking the will of God even while pursuing our own needs:

"But seek His kingdom

and His righteousness,

and all these things

will be given to you . . ."

MATTHEW 6:31–33

We are also assured that no matter what we endure, we can be confident that

"And we know

that for those who love God

all things work together for good, for those

who are called according to His purpose."

ROMANS 8:28 (ESV)

The promise of the Kingdom to come transcends the problems we may face here on earth. The parable of the rich man and Lazarus (Luke 16:19–31), highlights this point.

The poor man, Lazarus, who sat at the rich man's gate, with sores that were licked by the dogs, is a picture of abject misery. We would not wish that for ourselves or for any our dear ones. And the description of the rich man paints an enviable picture. Our society usually promotes the portrayal of the rich man as a picture of success. Yet Jesus revealed that in this account, Lazarus ended up in the bosom of Abraham, while the rich man languished in Hades!

Our situations and circumstances take on a different look when viewed through the lens of eternity. Absent that lens, we become shortsighted, self-seeking, and have a warped view of success. That pursuit of sham success prompts us to consider *How can I jockey my way to any available advantage?*

In *As You Like It*, William Shakespeare wrote,

> *"All the world's a stage,*
> *And all the men and women*
> *merely players . . ."* [20]

There is much truth in that saying. Particularly important is the realization that we are merely the players of roles that we have been assigned. We are not the producer, the director, or scriptwriter of our lives, though we may wish we were or may act like we are. In many serial productions, the players often do not know what the subsequent episodes will include, let alone if their role will continue in them. They just play their role the best they can and let the powers that be decide their part, if any, in the following episode.

Here's a thought: If we follow His directions and play our part accordingly, not only will we have an effective life here, but we will also, more importantly, be enrolled in the sequel that is to follow: "the eternal life."

So, when we come before God in prayer, let us not be preoccupied with our own agenda. Instead, let us sincerely seek the agenda set by Him.

I remember, while in elementary school, participating in basic drills. The simplest exercise was to stand at attention (did they mean "at tension"?) or to be at ease. Though being at ease allowed one to be more relaxed, it did not permit us to slouch off. It required us at a moment's notice to be ready to come to attention.

Similar drills are also part of the discipline of military personnel. Consider being a private in the Army and appearing before a high-ranking general, awaiting orders for the day. Even if we were asked to be at ease, would we dare be sloppy, distracted, tell the general about the various ways in which we wished to indulge ourselves, or instruct him to carry out our wishes for us? Or would we wait patiently, ready to do his bidding to the best of our ability?

Coming into the presence of God the Father in prayer is many times more awe-inspiring than appearing before any Army general. Let's remember that each time we pray, we are ushered into the presence of the Creator and Ruler of the universe. Yet we are also afforded the privilege of being there as our Father's child.

So how do we facilitate what we profess: "Your kingdom come; Your will be done"? We do so by ceding ourselves and our kingdoms to His Kingdom, seeking to be led by His Spirit, so that our will is subject to His. King David's conclusion of Psalm 139 captures this very aptly:

"Search me, God,
and know my heart;
test me and know my anxious thoughts.
See if there is any offensive way in me,
and lead me in the way everlasting."

PSALM 139:23–24 NIV

Failing businesses with potential are often taken over by more successful businesses. Even businesses that seem to be humming along nicely can also be taken over to enhance their profitability. Let us remember that even when we may not see any satisfactory options for our lives or our kingdoms, He who is in the salvaging, redeeming, and restoring business sees potential for our lives in His Kingdom and seeks to lead us in the everlasting way!

Please note that God is not in the business of hostile take-overs. He is always willing to take over but never without our consent. He is ever patient and always waiting. Shall we respond to Jesus when he says,

"Here I am,

I stand at the door and knock.

If anyone hears my voice

and opens the door,

I will come in

and eat with that person,

and they with me."

REVELATION 3:20

When I was a young boy, my brother Joe taught me to play chess. He was much better than I and could easily defeat me. Sometimes, I would want to give up as soon as I lost a valuable piece or two. But I recall occasions when Joe would make me an unusual offer.

When I was ready to give up, he would offer to turn the chessboard around and play with my pieces (in what I considered a hopeless position) while allowing me to play with his pieces in the seemingly superior position. And the remarkable outcome was that Joe would often still win!

Shall we yield our kingdoms and our will to the one who can best turn losing situations into winning ones?

RECAP

In the first two verses of this prayer, we feel invited into the Father's presence by Jesus and adopted into His family. Having accepted God as our Father (He adopts us as His children when we accept Jesus as His son), we see ourselves as members of His household. When we accept this offer, no matter what our past has been, we are exalted and transformed into princes and princesses in the Kingdom of Heaven. Jesus's Father has become our Father too. We have become part of the greater "Body of Christ." Citizenship in Heaven is conferred on us.

Remember, our stay on earth is a temporary posting. We see Heaven as our eventual home and are mindful of exalting and glorifying our Father's name at *all* times.

As members of His Kingdom, we yield our paltry kingdoms to our Father to manage as part of His Kingdom. We want to stop our kingdom from rivaling His. The Holy Spirit comes alongside us to be our counselor and ever-present guide. We learn to subject our will to His, seeking justice and mercy, especially for God's beloved constituency of the needy and have-nots, while we practice walking humbly in His presence. As children of our heavenly Father, we commit to being aligned with His will by frequently checking with the Holy Spirit's feedback and redirection when we go astray. We are aware the Holy Spirit provides us a Spiritual Positioning System (SPS), and we undertake to utilize it regularly.

CHAPTER 5

GIVE US THIS DAY OUR DAILY BREAD

A sking to be given anything is always humbling. It makes us aware that we need or want something that we do not have. It reminds us that we are not self-sufficient. And that whoever we are asking for something from has the power to decide whether or not to grant us our request.

Charles Spurgeon likened "Give us this day our daily bread" to a beggar's plea. In his analysis of the utterances in this prayer, Spurgeon outlined the different roles represented in different verses:

Our Father in Heaven:
CHILD AWAY FROM HOME

Hallowed be your name:
WORSHIPER

Your Kingdom come:
SUBJECT

Your will be done on earth as it is in Heaven:
SERVANT

Give us this day our daily bread:
BEGGAR

Forgive us our debts as we forgive our debtors:
SINNER

Lead us not into temptation:
SINNER AT RISK OF BEING A

But deliver us from evil:
GREATER SINNER STILL

Spurgeon likened this entire prayer to a ladder which we descend stepwise from our uplifted roles at the beginning, to our baser roles by the end of the prayer.[21] That makes us recognize our dependence on God.

The English translation of this verse can sometimes sound more demanding than entreating in tone. It can even sound brash and entitled, perhaps, like the prodigal son who asked for his share of the inheritance. The Berean Literal Bible presents this verse as "*Grant* us this day our daily bread," which captures the more appropriate sentiment.[22] But "*Give* us . . ." is by far the most common and accepted translation. Some also consider that "Give us" sounds more straightforward and childlike in asking the Father to meet a need or want.

As we feast on this very rich verse in the context of the prayer thus far, we find ourselves as recently adopted members of Jesus's family. We also have embarked on a mission to herald His Kingdom and carry out His will. In pursuing this mission, we take our cue from Jesus himself, who stated his purpose:

"For the Son of Man
came to seek and to save the lost."

LUKE 19:10

Our mission (consistent with the Great Commission) effectively enrolls us in His team, His army—an unconventional army that always seeks to search and rescue but never to harm or destroy. Being enrolled in that mission gives us the right to expect that He will provide bread for our needs.

"Daily bread" obviously signifies more than just literal bread. Bread includes all provisions needed for living— our sustenance.

If we totally belong to Him, He is responsible for us. But our insecurity often leads us to doubt whether He will really provide for us and meet all our needs. That insecurity prompts us to devote our efforts and energies toward trying to provide for ourselves and our own kingdoms.

We spend much of our lives trying to *not* be dependent on God. We strive to provide for our needs and the needs of our dependents (our kingdoms), for today and for the near future. And, if we can, a cushion for the distant future too! For many of us, our education was geared to equip us to compete in the marketplace of life. That has facilitated employment or home-making, which provides and cares for us and ours. We even store up for times when we may no longer be able to continue providing for ourselves or for unforeseen circumstances.

But Jesus urged dependence on him and his Father. In the same chapter in which this prayer, taught by Jesus, is record-ed, the Gospel of Matthew quotes Jesus teaching his followers:

"Look at the birds of the air,

they do not sow or reap or store away in barns,

and yet your heavenly Father feeds them.

Are you not much more valuable than they?"

MATTHEW 6:26

Now, if we were on duty in the army, we would expect the army to provide our daily food. Even when we are on assign-ment from nonmilitary businesses, we expect to be provided our food or given allowances to cover expenses for it. Sim-ilarly, while we are about our Father's business, we can ex-pect that He will provide for our daily needs. It is also worth noting that the provision is for a day at a time. Per diem! We usually want to be shown a long-term plan and to be provid-ed assurances for the future. This prayer teaches us to change our perspective to *one day at a time*. It teaches us to be totally dependent on Him against the backdrop of the assurance of eternity with Him.

Reflecting on the source of our "bread," we realize that everything we have (including that which we think we have gotten by ourselves) comes from Him. When we hear of others like us who abruptly lost their sustenance for whatever reason, "Give us this day our daily bread" reinforces the recognition of our dependence on our Father.

From a biblical perspective, "daily bread," of course, reminds us of the Israelites receiving *mana* while they were in the wilderness. Mana was a wafer-like bread which seemed to miraculously appear like dried dew every morning; it fed the multitudes for years. The particulars of this bread was that it was only good for that day. It was new every morning. If kept over until the following day, it would spoil, except on the Sabbath, when it stayed good for the second day.

Think of the hundreds of thousands of Israelites traversing the wilderness without food of their own but being provided mana every morning for bread. And that wasn't for just a day or two. It went on for forty years! No wonder that one of the names that the Israelites had for God was *Jehovah Jireh*, (Lord God who provides). But that is not surprising when we remember that this same miracle-working Father enabled Jesus to feed five thousand men with five loaves and two fish (see Matthew 14:13–21). And they even picked up twelve baskets of excess food. And the gospels tell us that Jesus fed another four thousand men with seven loaves on a different occasion too (see Mark 8:1–10; Matthew 15:32–39).

While writing this book, I have felt like the boy who handed over the few loaves and two fish, which the Lord multiplied. My few pages are being handed over for the Lord to bless, multiply, and feed His children as He sees appropriate.

One of the characteristics of God that we begin to appreciate is that He is a God who multiplies. From giant stars to the tiniest cells, from flora and fauna to humans, He has instituted multiplication into all that He created. He is indeed a God who brings forth plentifully.

And this same miracle-working Father is at work even today.

A more recent and noteworthy example is that of George Muller in Bristol, England, who took care of thousands of orphans in the nineteenth century. It is awe inspiring to read about an instance when the children were at the breakfast table before going to school. They prayed, giving thanks before the meal like they usually did, except that there was no food on the table nor in the kitchen. They also did not have any money to buy food. But just then, there was a knock on the door; a baker presented a cartload of bread that he had felt prompted to bake for the orphans. A few minutes later, a milkman dropped off several pails of milk because his cart had unexpectedly broken down next to the orphanage. On another occasion, George Muller, having run out of money to support the children, received a significant sum of money in the mail, sent a month previously from overseas, that arrived just in the nick of time! [23]

There are very many more instances of God coming through to meet the needs at George Muller's orphanage while they were totally dependent on Him.

In the early 1970s, Taiichi Ohno, an industrial engineer employed by Toyota in Japan, was credited with having developed "Just in Time" (JIT) technology to streamline inventory and the supply of necessary parts. This provides for just enough parts or raw materials to be made available as are necessary for the manufacture of an item, without the burden of ordering and storing excess amounts.[24] The previous practice was found to require much more capital and storage space, while also contributing to waste. Today, virtually all major manufacturers and assembly line productions use JIT technology to enhance productivity and minimize waste. But our Father has been orchestrating "just in time" sequences for His children who rely on Him all through the ages.

It takes faith to believe that God would provide for our needs on a regular basis. If we are responding to His call, He will provide for us. We are not assured that we will be *shown* the provisions for the future ahead of time. But He is faithful and will never be found wanting. To believe that requires faith.

> *"Now faith is the assurance*
> *of things hoped for,*
> *the conviction of things not seen."*

The provision of "bread from heaven" takes on additional significance when we note that Jesus described himself as "the bread that came down from heaven" (John 6:35–58). Mana was a shadow[25] (a forerunner of what was to come) of the true bread that was to come down from Heaven. He is our sustenance. Once again, this prayer brings us back to Jesus.

"You are what you eat" is an adage attributed to the French gastronomist Jean Brillat-Savarin in 1826.[26] That referred to our bodies. What we feed our mind also determines how our minds turn out to be. It makes sense, if our goal is to be more like Jesus, to feed on him and his word every day. He needs to become the staple diet for our minds. How significant then that Jesus also instituted the sacrament of the Eucharist during the Last Supper with his disciples. (It is commemorated as Holy Communion or the Lord's Supper.) He took bread, gave thanks to the Father, broke it, and gave it to his disciples, saying, "This is my body which is given for you." We, his disciples, are invited to eat what he offered, and, as his followers who are part of his living body, be ready for our bodies also to be broken for the benefit of others.

When we consider needing bread for our earthly sustenance, it can be a vital need, met by many kinds of "bread." When we consider needing bread for our eternal sustenance, there is only one bread that meets that need the bread that came down from Heaven, Jesus Christ, our Lord. And he willingly offers himself to all who need and want him.

In regenerative medicine, stem cell therapy has emerged as a promising area of research and treatment.[27] Every human starts out as a single-celled fertilized ovum called a "zygote." The zygote then divides into two, which divides yet again and again; in the process, the number of cells multiplies. The newborn baby has about 26 billion cells. The cell multiplication continues into adulthood, by which time we have about 100 trillion cells. The genetic code in the zygote determines how the body is formed and how cells differentiate to form our various organs and tissues. Human stem cells are special pre-differentiated cells with the potential to develop into many different cell types. We are truly fearfully and wonderfully made.

In certain conditions in which there is damage to the cells, tissues, or organs which cannot otherwise be treated, it has been found that introducing stem cells (cells from an earlier stage of development) allows for those cells to multiply and form new tissues with the functions of the damaged body part.

Think of a branch of a plant being damaged, diseased, or pruned; the stem has the ability to generate another branch. Similarly, stem cells can generate specialized cells that restore, to varying degrees, the function of the damaged body part. People with leukemia, lymphoma, Parkinson's disease, Type 1 diabetes, spinal cord injuries, etc., are among those who are being helped significantly by stem cell therapy.

Jesus is called the Alpha and the Omega, the beginning and

the end *(see* Revelation 1:8, 21:6, 22:13*)*. The Gospel of John also starts with the description of Jesus as the Word who was with God—and was God—from the very beginning (see John 1:1). He is mankind's stem cell! The cure for man, who has gone wrong or become spiritually sick with no other available cure, is to receive a form of stem cell transplant by introducing Jesus into the spiritually sick individual. The Eucharist delivers Jesus to us in the form of bread and wine, as his body and blood ("This is my body; This is my blood"). Some of staunch faith accept this literally; some others, of equally staunch faith, consider it merely symbolic. As Jesus said,

> *"According to your faith*
> *let it be done to you."*

MATTHEW 9:29

It can be mind-boggling for us to figure out how Jesus could give himself to the very many who seek him, day after day, for thousands of years. Perhaps, the mana for the thousands of Israelites for forty years, and the feeding of the five thousand (and the four thousand) was to allow us to marvel at and recognize that He who created man can also create what man needs for sustenance out of nothing—both for the body and the spirit.

We have been designed to naturally hunger for food, and, when we have eaten the food, it satisfies us and replenishes us. But Jesus had a radically different view of food.

> *"My food,"*
> *said Jesus,*
> *"is to do the will of Him who sent me*
> *and to finish His work."*

JOHN 4:34

Here again, we see the salience of pursuing the will of the Father. Through this prayer, we are tutored to hunger for and feed on "the bread that came down from heaven." Then, we too can be satisfied, replenished, and do the will of the Father, thereby bringing the Kingdom of Heaven here on earth.

CHAPTER 6

AND FORGIVE US OUR DEBTS AS WE ALSO HAVE FORGIVEN OUR DEBTORS

In 1526, William Tyndale presented the first translation of the New Testament into English from Greek and the Latin Vulgate. This verse in that translation read "Forgive us our trespasses as we forgive those who trespass against us."[28] That translation of the verse also continued to remain in the *Book of Common Prayer.*[29] Those of us who are older may be familiar with (and may have even memorized) this particular translation, which is worthy of consideration.

One is guilty of a trespass when one enters a property without consent or goes where one is not authorized to go.

The Disney movie *The Lion King* has an excellent illustration that sheds light on this issue.[30] The young lion cub, Simba, heir to the Pridelands kingdom, is instructed by his father, Mufasa, never to venture into the "shadowy place" at the border of the Pridelands. But young Simba is intrigued, and curiosity gets the better of him. He sneaks into the shadowy place to see for himself against the expressed directions of his father. That leads to a whole series of problems and attempts at solutions, which is the storyline of the movie. Though this is a children's movie with animal characters, it also resonates with adults because of the analogies to choices and consequences in human lives.

Instead of heeding the counsel of our Father, we let curiosity or other attractive lures (temptations) lead us into dangerous areas with adverse consequences. Sometimes, we don't even see the consequences as adverse and continue our aberrant course until much later, or, sometimes, even never.

The account of events in the Garden of Eden brings this into focus. We read that Adam and Eve were instructed not to eat of the fruit of the tree in the middle of the garden. But their curiosity was aroused. The temptation that their eyes would be opened and that they would be like God led them to act contrary to the injunction of God.

We all have an unfounded confidence that we know better. We are tempted to believe that if we are presented with right and wrong choices, we can distinguish between them ourselves and will always choose the right option. Human history, as well as each of our own histories, clearly says otherwise.

Indeed, the core problem with us is that in our minds, we choose to go where we ought not to go. We trespass by going into the "shadowy places" against the counsel of our Father. We are often driven by some lure or our curiosity to check it out simply because it is there.

In a telling and candid confession by former president Bill Clinton during a CBS interview with Dan Rather, when asked about why he engaged in the indiscretions that tarnished his presidency, the President replied, "Just because I could."[31]

That is true of all of us. From King David (who had serious indiscretions, even though he is described in the Bible as a man after God's own heart) to the least of us, we err simply because we can. Disregarding the counsel of God, we are prone to explore whatever we can. And thereby, err. That then leads to our need for forgiveness. As the saying goes, "To err is human; to forgive, divine."

Tyndale's translation identifies the underlying issue as our willingness to trespass in our minds and pursue our own counsel rather than to abide within where God permits us. We choose to enter forbidden territories.

Psalm 91 begins with

"Whoever dwells in the shelter of the Most High
will rest in the shadow of the Almighty."

That can be seen not only as a Biblical assurance but also as a command. Within the shadow of the Almighty are the safe dwelling places. If we desire the shelter of the Most High, we may not venture beyond where we are covered by His shadow. We may not allow the lure of the other attractions or the fear of missing out on something that may "open our eyes" to cause us to stray into perilous areas.

What does anybody need forgiveness for? Our legalistic mindset thinks of actions that have been errant and constitute offenses deserving of censure and punishment. Instead, let us consider that that we offend God primarily whenever we abandon His will and pursue our own. Whatever subsequently results from that aberration is secondary.

In law, *mens rea* is the Latin term for the principle which posits that, in some cases, to be found guilty of serious crimes, it must be proven that the offender *intended* to do wrong. The intent is at the core of what is held against a person for whatever unlawful acts they committed.

Actus reus (guilty act) refers to the unlawful act that follows from mens rea (guilty mind). We often tend to focus on the act, but the underlying mental process that leads to the act is where the offense is truly birthed.

Jesus expounded on this in the Sermon on the Mount, when he stressed that looking lustfully at a person is equivalent to committing adultery, and harboring anger is equivalent to committing murder (see Matthew 5:21–28).

So what we need forgiveness for—and healing from —is our wandering minds that go astray and trespass into unhealthy and unsafe territories. The permissive culture that we live in persistently aids and abets us by suggesting that the unsafe shadowy places are really worth exploring, that others are doing so, and that we would be missing out if we didn't go there.

Acknowledging that, let us return to the more prevalent translation, that of "forgive us our *debts*."

Do we really owe God a debt? Have we taken from God and not paid it back?

To grasp that, we need to look back at the previous phrase in this prayer: "Give us this day our daily bread," which, in turn, feeds off the verse that preceded it. Once we accepted the fatherhood of God, we became princely subjects of His Kingdom. We then undertook to become outposts[32] of His Kingdom and subject our will to His, here on earth. Once enrolled in His service, we had the right to expect that He would provide us our daily bread. We got to eat at His table. We remained on His payroll. But, having received daily bread from our Father, the real question is whether we have served His Kingdom.

We acknowledged earlier, that in our earthly lives, the main rival to our Father's Kingdom is our own kingdom. Have we taken His bread and tried to promote the rival kingdom instead of His? Have we been pursuing our interests, of which He does not approve, on His time? If so, we have very significant debts to repay (a lifetime's worth)—debts that we simply cannot repay.

All of us have fallen short. And we all need His forgiveness. Thankfully, He is a forgiving God. The ransom for us was paid by the death of Jesus on the cross at Calvary. It is the price that Jesus willingly paid to have us in His Kingdom. Talking of debts, how do we repay a debt to the one who died to save us?

Mosaic law had established the practice of substitutionary

sacrifice to seek forgiveness. Depending on affordability and circumstances, a bull, a ram, a goat, a lamb, or a dove was sacrificed after the offense, or sin of an individual or the community, was ceremonially transposed on to the animal. Animals without apparent blemish were selected to have higher value as the substitute. The substitutionary killing of the animal without blemish was then seen as effecting justice. In so doing, the conventionally accepted price was considered to have been paid for forgiveness. As we can see, a good specimen of a *lesser* creature was sacrificed to absolve and preserve the life of the human, who was clearly viewed as a *higher* creature.

On the cross, Jesus consented to his own death as *the* substitutionary sacrifice. But in this case, it was the sacrifice of the infinitely higher *creator,* Jesus the Son (one with the Father), to save the lower *creature,* man. Jesus became the sacrificial lamb that takes away the sin of the world! Jesus's willingness to always abide by the will of God, his Father, even to the point of death, rendered him perfect and without blemish. The cleansing value to the creature (man), of the unblemished creator, who became incarnate to be offered as a substitutionary sacrifice, is *infinite.* Hence the ability for that *one* sacrifice of Jesus to atone for the sins of *all* the world.

Having been granted this high-priced forgiveness, we are being asked to also forgive others. Because there is no room for bitterness, resentment, or unforgiveness in His Kingdom. That baggage is not permitted in the Kingdom of Heaven, nor is anybody with that baggage allowed in. So, if we are to enter and remain in His Kingdom, not only must we be forgiven our own debts, we must also forgive everyone else their debts, if any, to us.

What debts do others owe us? After all, with what did we come into this world? Anything that we have or have accumulated is not really our own. Can we really insist that we are owed anything by anybody?

It is true that we have all been offended by others to different degrees. By what was done to us (their actions), they may even come to be seen as our enemies. But Jesus commands us to love our enemies. Jesus himself demonstrated that by praying for those who were crucifying him to be forgiven, even while they were in the act. Lest we think that those were misguided people unlike us, let us recognize that all of us have either rejected or repeatedly betrayed Jesus, and we are those for whom he needed to die to enable our entry into His Kingdom. It was the incomprehensible, astounding love that led Jesus to come and be our atoning sacrifice while we were still sinners and "enemies of God." So how much of a debt do we owe for Jesus's sacrifice that enables us entry into the Kingdom of Heaven?

> *"For if, while we were God's enemies,*
> *we were reconciled to him*
> *through the death of his Son,*
> *how much more, having been reconciled,*
> *shall we be saved through his life!"*

ROMANS 5:10 NIV

There is no denying our "woundedness." Absent forgiveness, we remain stuck in our woundedness.

Think about this: Will any amount of punishment make a past wrong right? Today, if we haven't forgiven the ones who had hurt us badly and who, to us, seem undeserving of forgiveness, who is it that feels the most hurt? They or us? We may refuse to forgive because we are still hurt, but we will hurt more because we haven't forgiven!

Forgiveness is a necessary cleansing for our wellbeing. Forgiveness is also a prerequisite for the kingdom of our Father. Jesus particularly emphasized this right after teaching the disciples this prayer:

"For if you forgive other people when they sin against you,
your heavenly Father will also forgive you.
But if you do not forgive others their sins,
your Father will not forgive your sins."

MATTHEW 6:14–15

Jesus also expanded on this in the parable of the unforgiving servant, which emphasizes this very message.

Therefore, the kingdom of heaven is like a king who wanted to settle accounts with his servants. As he began the settlement, a man who owed him ten thousand bags of gold was brought to him. Since he was not able to pay, the master ordered that he and his wife and children and all that he had be sold to repay the debt. At this the servant fell on his knees before him.

"Be patient with me," he begged, "and I will pay back everything." The servant's master took pity on him, canceled the debt, and let him go.

But when that servant went out, he found one of his fellow servants who owed him a hundred silver coins. He grabbed him and began to choke him. "Pay back what you owe me!" he demanded.

His fellow servant fell to his knees and begged him, "Be patient with me, and I will pay it back."

But he refused. Instead, he went off and had the man thrown into prison until he could pay the debt. When the other servants saw what had happened, they were outraged and went and told their master everything that had happened.

Then the master called the servant in. "You wicked servant," he said, "I canceled all that debt of yours because you begged me to. Shouldn't you have had mercy on your fellow servant just as I had on you?" In anger, his master handed him over to the jailers to be tortured, until he should pay back all he owed.

"This is how my heavenly Father
will treat each of you unless you forgive
your brother or sister from your heart."

MATTHEW 18:23–35

We all get offended and bear grudges because we have been hurt. Our sense of fairness demands that our hurt be balanced out by equivalent hurt to whoever offended us.

When hurt ferments, it leads to intent to harm in any way we can (e.g., Cain toward Abel, the brothers toward Joseph, Saul toward David, Herod toward John the Baptist, the Chief Priests toward Jesus, etc.). Our daily news is usually full of instances of retributive harm for perceived hurts by individuals, groups of people, and even by nations.

All of us carry with us burdens of guilt, shame, bitterness, and resentment. It takes forgiveness to melt those burdens away and become more Christ-like. Forgiveness can also be understood as amnesty. Amnesty is derived from the Greek word "amnesia" (now part of the English lexicon), which means "to remember it no more." Forgiveness involves remembering it no more. Without forgiveness, we keep regurgitating the shame, guilt, bitterness, and resentment, and that keeps our lives mired in a miserable existence.

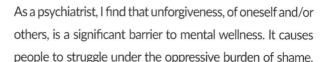

As a psychiatrist, I find that unforgiveness, of oneself and/or others, is a significant barrier to mental wellness. It causes people to struggle under the oppressive burden of shame, depression, anxiety, anger, and unrelenting dissatisfaction.

Recognition that the price for heavenly forgiveness was paid for us in full by Jesus on the cross (while we remained so undeserving of it) allows us to partially grasp the extent of the love and grace extended to us. It is when we truly realize that we have received encompassing mercy as well as grace that we are able to extend mercy and grace to those who have hurt us deeply.

Being mindful of our heavenly citizenship is also vital to forgiveness.

Consider this. What from earth matters in Heaven? Certainly, no worldly possessions. When the goalpost is Heaven, earthly belongings lose significance.

"If anyone wants to sue you

and take your shirt,

hand over your coat as well"

MATTHEW 5:40

As for our perceived worldly position, none of our titles, qualifications, or reputations matter either. Realize that the perceptions of our own image or standing, over which we may have lost much sleep, are totally inconsequential. (Ironically, much of our woundedness most often stems from perceived injuries to our image in our earthly lives.)

But, as Jesus cautioned, the order in the Kingdom of Heaven is much different from how it is on earth.

"Indeed there are those who are last

who will be first,

and first who will be last."

LUKE 13:30

The only thing that truly matters is how Jesus-like we are in yielding to the will of the Father. Sanctification, as has been stated, is the process of making us more like Jesus. It is a long process in which the Holy Spirit chisels and transforms our nature to get it to respond to the circumstances we face with the love and compassion that Jesus displayed. At the Last Supper with his disciples, on the eve of his crucifixion, Jesus washed their feet (including Judas's, knowing that he would betray him that night) and instructed them to do likewise (see John 13:1–15).

We need forgiveness for all the ways we are "*un*-Jesus-like." In the early 1990s, the term "WWJD" was made popular by the revival of the Rev. Charles Sheldon's book *In His Steps: What Would Jesus Do?* originally written in 1896. It prompts us to consider what Jesus would have done in the circumstances that we face.[33] It helps that the Spirit in us is the same Spirit that was in Jesus and faithfully prompts us to do what Jesus would do. Every time.

It has been said that forgiveness is the only accepted currency on the turnstile to enter His Kingdom. We follow him who was rejected, reviled, spat upon, falsely accused, betrayed, slapped, beaten, scourged, crucified, and yet . . . he forgave them all. We are recipients of his mercy and grace. So how can we be followers of Jesus and not forgive those who have offended us?

RECAP

We have a new identity. We have been elevated to become children of God the Father. We have been granted citizenship in Heaven, our eventual home. We undertake to always hallow and honor the name of God, our Father. Our longing for God's Kingdom leads us to make our lives an outpost of His Kingdom here on earth. We do so by accepting His presence, His sovereignty, and being totally yielded to His will.

In our desire to be more like Jesus, we gratefully feed on his provision, his word, and his broken but undying body that we may do likewise. He is our stem cell who replaces the old and flawed with the new and pure.

We admit that we have strayed from His will. We have sought to promote our own kingdoms and neglected His. We have trespassed in our minds into territories of which our Father does not approve. We therefore ask for and receive forgiveness for going astray through the atoning sacrifice of Jesus the creator for us, the creature. We also choose to forgive all who wounded and offended us. Forgiveness cleanses and restores us, giving us the opportunity to be more Jesus-like henceforth, guided by the Holy Spirit.

CHAPTER 7

Lead Us Not into Temptation

The end of the previous verse places us on a very comfortable perch. As the recap on the previous page highlights, we have a new identity and a new citizenship as members of the family of God the Father and citizens of the Kingdom of Heaven. As outposts of His Kingdom, we sought to be totally yielded to His will. For falling way short of our calling, we asked for and received forgiveness. We also forgave all who wounded and offended us. We receive stem cell infusions of Jesus, who makes us whole. That puts us in the most desirable situation: cleansed, well-fed, forgiven, replenished, accepting God's will, and delighting in being in the Kingdom of God the Father as His children.

But this also leaves us vulnerable!

Vulnerable, because we feel we are on the verge of messing up and falling off this enviable perch. Vulnerable, because even though we want to be yielded to Him and His will, *we* still have to exercise the choices regarding all the decisions of our lives. And that is where we risk going astray.

That brings us to the core of the problem that mankind faces. What determines the choices we make? Even for those of us who wish to abide by our Father's will, we find it to be a struggle.

Though we may wish to feed on what our Father gives us, we also invariably feed on what the world around us heaps on us. And far too often, the pull of the world prevails. We find ourselves in the driver's seat, with decision-making responsibilities at numerous crossroads in our lives. Even though the Holy Spirit is available as our copilot or navigator, we still have to execute *all* the decisions of our life. We know from our own life histories that our decision-making has been suspect in the past and could be again.

There is a plea of desperation in this verse. A recognition that, knowing ourselves, we know we will succumb to temptation. Unless the Holy Spirit expertly leads us through the many crossroads of our lives, we are bound to mess up. In the beloved Psalm of David, he wrote,

"Your rod and your staff, they comfort me."

PSALM 23:4

We need both the guidance of the staff that leads as well as the disciplining correction of the rod that follows to ensure that we stay on the right path.

It takes disciplining to make the disciple.

Upon reflection, I now see the benefit of the corrections that I have received in my life. I am comforted to know that He cares enough for me to use the rod to ensure that I safely make it to His Kingdom. Psalm 139:5 also reinforces the same sentiment:

"You hem me in—behind and before,
you have laid your hand upon me."

All the Synoptic Gospels mention the temptations that Jesus was beset with soon after his baptism (see Matthew 4:1–10; Mark 1:12–13; Luke 4:1–13). The three temptations which are specified may be representative of overall temptations, since Jesus was reportedly there, being tempted for all of forty days. Let's look at each of the three and their application to our lives and circumstances.

The first temptation put to Jesus was to use his power to turn stones into bread to feed his hunger. If you are tempted to chuckle at this, it is understandable. He who is the bread of Heaven, who would miraculously feed thousands, was being tempted to make bread from stones. Jesus responded by being proper and quoting scripture: "Man does not live on bread alone, but on every word that comes from the mouth of God" (Matthew 4:4).

A great temptation that we all face is to feed our many appetites, using everything in our power and at our disposal to satisfy them, simply because it *feels* good. Behavioral sciences tell us that the more we satisfy our appetites, the stronger they become, even to the point of addiction. Food, drink, drugs, and sex are easily identified, but we are at risk of seeking gratification through stimulation of any kind. In recent decades, for example, addiction to information, gaming, and social media inputs have consumed and overpowered so many among us, especially our young ones. Everything that feels good gets reinforced, making it more likely that we will engage in those pursuits again.

We are all thrill seekers or, at least, satisfaction seekers. We are at risk of going back to engage in whatever was thrilling or satisfying in preference to what we may be aware of as the will of God, which, at that point in time, can seem comparably unexciting. In fact, in the vicinity of an anticipated thrill, the will of God might not even enter into consideration because the intensity of the anticipated satisfaction can be overpowering and consume our total attention.

In the second reported temptation, the devil dares Jesus to throw himself down from the steeple of the temple to see if the angels would hold him up as promised in Psalm 91:11–12. Jesus responded with a rebuttal; he again quoted scripture, saying that we are not to put the Lord God to test (see Deuteronomy 6:16).

We all face temptations to engage in various risk-taking

behaviors across all areas of our lives. Speeding, neglecting our health, procrastination, cutting corners, behaving differently when no one is watching, and "white lies" are simple examples. We often get away with what we may consider to be minor infractions.

Psychologists Neil Weinstein and Tali Sharot have separately shed light on the "optimism bias" that contributes to risk-taking behaviors. They explain how we overestimate the likelihood of encountering positive events and how we incorrectly anticipate favorable outcomes.[34,35] It causes us to believe that we can get away with lapses and infractions . . . that "our luck will hold out." When we do get away with it, our errant behavior is reinforced. We then expect that we will continue to get away with such infractions in the future.

Believers have been known to thank God for letting them get away with such errant behavior. They may even consider it the grace of God—an undeserved favor from God. Sometimes, such grace from God is even assumed and appropriated. This, not surprisingly, results in repeated and still greater risk-taking behaviors until adverse consequences eventually catch up with us. Unwarranted appropriations of grace most often bring about disgrace!

Even those (perhaps, *especially* those) who think they have discovered their godly groove and are experiencing a blessed life need to be cautious. In recent decades, many stalwarts of faith have succumbed to temptations, which, when exposed, have caused much of their erstwhile good work to suffer disrepute.

The third recorded temptation was for Jesus to be offered possession of all the earthly kingdoms if he worshipped the devil. Jesus, of course, spurned that offer. What are earthly kingdoms when compared to the Kingdom of Heaven? And Jesus once again quoted scripture: "You shall worship the Lord your God, and him only shall you serve" (Luke 4:8 ESV).

The lure of possessions and fame remains a major temptation for most people to use their gifts and talents in pursuits not aligned with the will of God the Father. The stature, recognition, adulation, and comforts that they could provide are rewards that can be highly reinforcing and enticing while also deflecting us from His Kingdom and His will. Once again, that to which we resonate has the power to steer us and effectively trap us.

Consider any game with its respective rules and proficiencies. It is understandably inviting to pit our skills against those of our peers. It is gratifying, especially if we are any good at it. The better we get at these challenges, the greater our investment in these activities to get even better. Our competitive juices gush forth, and much of our lives can be consumed by them. We even vicariously live through the exploits of expert players or of our favorite teams. It is not uncommon for people to have multiple sporting interests, fed by television and online access, available around the clock. The same often applies even to aspects of our work or just continually feeding on information.

Is this harmful? Not in the conventional sense of the term. But, when we consider that these diversions may be detours that steer us away from a potentially better course for our lives, the opportunity costs can be significant. Once again, let us look at the Parable of the Rich Man and Lazarus (Luke 16:19–31). The rich man seemed to be winning, hands down, wasn't he? Or was he? Jesus asked,

> *"What good is it for someone*
> *to gain the whole world,*
> *yet forfeit their soul?"*

MARK 6:36

No one is immune to the lures of worldly attractions and rewards. Consider what we feel we are good at: a job, a hobby, a sport, a talent, or any abilities for which others appreciate us. That which we spend most of our time doing will probably indicate our greatest interests and passions. Whom does it please more? Ourselves or our Father?

Engaging with Jesus through His word and Spirit introduced us to His Father's Kingdom and added a heavenly dimension to our lives. That heavenly dimension grows as we follow Him and follow through the process of sanctification. But we never lose our worldly dimension, which the apostle Paul referred to as "flesh," as long as we live here on earth. He highlighted that struggle:

"For I do not do the good that I want to do, but the evil I do not want to do—this I keep on doing."

ROMANS 7:19

Our decisional choices are subject to both the prompts of the Holy Spirit as well as our own worldly impulses, which often seem louder. We are therefore at risk of yielding to our worldly counsel. That is what led to us needing forgiveness to begin with.

Left to ourselves and the things of the world that we resonate to, we will go astray, *repeatedly*. Hence the desperate plea: Lead us not into temptation. This verse does not suggest that, otherwise, our Father would lead us into temptation. It recognizes that without His leading, we would invariably succumb to temptation.

"I Am Second," a multimedia movement about putting Jesus first, that was founded in 2012 in Dallas-Fort Worth. It initially targeted the local area with testimonials of celebrities as well as regular people. Its powerful message led to a national and international following. The underlying message is ever true, though, like most movements, it takes significant volunteerism or continued financial investment to sustain attention in our fiercely competitive world.[36]

In February 2009, *Smithsonian Magazine* carried an article about the mouth of the Columbia River in Oregon.[37] That is considered to be one of the most treacherous harbor entrances on the planet (especially during a storm) and has even been called the "Graveyard of the Pacific." But big ships with very valuable cargo are guided through these dangerous waters by expert pilots, who come on board specifically to navigate them through this perilous zone. The captains of those big ships do not attempt that section of their journey without the expertise of these specialized pilots. That's a direct parallel to how we need the expertise of the Holy Spirit to guide us (except that our entire life is a perilous zone).

Our world provides a multitude of attractions to which we risk falling prey. They may all seem attractive to begin with. But, like the Trojan horse, they can eventually deceive and destroy us.

A hypothesis, not without merit, is that Satan (the contrarian angel who was cast out of Heaven) was out to demonstrate that God made a mistake by granting man free will. Satan's contention (literally and figuratively, as the devil's advocate), perhaps, was that man would make choices based upon his own counsel and attractions rather than on the counsel of God through the Holy Spirit. Therefore, he criticized God's creation of man with free will as flawed and unwise!

God had a counter to that (though no explanation was due). Though man was created error-capable and therefore error-inevitable, His grace provides forgiveness (through the atoning sacrifice of Jesus, God the Son). And forgiven man, when sanctified, can seek and abide by God's will. When man chooses to resonate to the guidance of the Holy Spirit and pursues God's will, it vindicates God's creation of man with free will.

Clearly, there are lives that bear out both sides of that argument. To which side of that argument will our lives be a witness?

Currently, there are debates along similar lines about man's creation of systems with Artificial Intelligence (AI).

Land mines are explosive weapons concealed underground or camouflaged on the ground. They are designed to destroy or disable persons or equipment when they pass over or near the mines. Introduced during the First World War as a defense against tanks, they are still employed in battle zones. Many of these mines lie dormant for years and even decades. Sadly, they continue to take a toll in thousands of lives each year, most of them civilians. Temptations are like land mines. They can lead to destruction when activated. Their great danger lies in their ability to remain dormant for extended periods of time. All of the temptations we have ever given in to lie dormant, camouflaged, or below the surface, like land mines, with the potential to be reactivated. The understandable alarm in this verse is because the temptations are capable of destroying or disabling us. We need divine help to protect us from our temptations.

This provides an appropriate segue into the second half of this verse: "but deliver us from evil."

CHAPTER 8

BUT DELIVER US
FROM THE EVIL ONE

L et's spend a moment thinking about delivery. . . *any* delivery. Whether it is mail, pizza, flowers, gifts, groceries, or even a baby, who does the work of delivering the items? How much of the work is done by the item being delivered compared to the deliverer? Zilch versus all. That's worth remembering.

We live in a self-help culture. We are urged to strive to deliver ourselves from problem situations in which we find ourselves entangled. We can perhaps extricate ourselves from problem situations generated by others if we marshal sufficient resources to overcome those problems. But, if the problems rise out of issues within ourselves, we are incapable of resolving them without external help. There's good reasoning behind the first step of the Twelve Steps of Alcoholics Anonymous being the acceptance of one's powerlessness over alcohol and the unmanageability of our lives.[38]

At times, we may take comfort if our present state is not as bad as what it was before. But, if we are still entwined in the problem that arises within ourselves, we will never get rid of it ourselves. If we wrestle with evil within ourselves, it is worth pondering what the nature of the evil is that holds us captive.

We may soothe ourselves into believing that, in our sight, most of what we spend our lives doing is not evil because we typically do not intend to harm anyone else (with no malice aforethought). We may also think of evil being outside us or of the devil (doer of evil) being the evil one. We will address that later in this chapter.

But what if evil really is *within* us?

If God's way to live is the right way, what can be said of ways that are *not* God's ways? They lead us elsewhere. And anywhere away from God gets us lost. But, thankfully, our Lord, the Good Shepherd, seeks and saves the lost.

Just a play on the word, but "evil" is "live" spelled backward.

All of us have an inherent, self-seeking, and self-satisfying motivator. It is our default engine. It is what drives us, unless we respond to a higher calling. Even then, our base desires war against our desire to pursue the higher calling. The apostle Paul's confession, quoted in the previous chapter, bears repeating:

"For I do not do the good I want to do,

but the evil I do not want to do—this I keep on doing."

ROMANS 7:19

Our genes and our lived experiences have primed us to find some things attractive. In our default state, we are drawn toward them. As humans, we are wired to resonate to those stimuli and respond to them. We also seek more of those stimuli. The choices we make about where we direct our attention, what information we feed ourselves, and what we are motivated to re-experience are all influenced by that to which we resonate. The basic resonance breeds successive generations of resonances in us. Those resonances determine much of human behavior. It underlies simple as well as complex behaviors—behavior patterns, habits, and addiction. We are creatures of habit.

Willpower (a complex concept) can temporarily prevail

over a given instance of base desire, but it cannot eradicate the desire. That desire will lurk within us. Unwholesome desires roost as the resident evil within us. We need deliverance from the power of such evil within us. We cannot do so ourselves. This can present as a hopeless situation with no relief.

Once again, the apostle Paul articulates this frustration with "the flesh" as a follow up to the verse cited above:

> *"What a wretched man I am!*
> *Who will rescue me from this body*
> *which is subject to death?"*

ROMANS 7:24

Giving in to our base desires ultimately gets us to a point of wretchedness.

As an addiction specialist, one of the common statements I hear from those who have suffered the ravages of addiction is "I'm sick and tired of feeling sick and tired all the time. I'm ready to be done with this life!"

That is a good description of wretchedness.

The apostle Paul answered his own question in the verse that followed immediately after:

> *"Thanks be to God, who delivers me*
> *through Jesus Christ our Lord."*

ROMANS 7:25

In the body, in the flesh, we are all vulnerable and at risk of of remaining trapped in the resonances from our past. But we can be delivered and transformed by renewing our minds and utilizing our Spiritual Positioning System, providing us something far superior to resonate to: His word, His Spirit, and His abiding presence.

"Do not conform to

the pattern of this world,

but be transformed by

the renewing of your mind.

Then you will be able to test

and approve what God's will is—

his good, pleasing and perfect will."

ROMANS 12:2

That would take a miracle. The good news is that He is indeed a miracle worker, and each of us are proof to ourselves that he is our deliverer and our very own miracle worker.

"Therefore, if anyone is in Christ,

the new creation has come.

The old is gone, the new is here!"

2 CORINTHIANS 5:17

We are forgiven. We are cleansed. We are inhabited by the Spirit of the Living God. Jesus promised that he will never abandon us. He will be with us to the end of the age. We can pursue God's good, pleasing, and perfect will. We can align ourselves to His will and be totally yielded to Him. Remember, the Spirit whom we have access to is the same Spirit that raised Jesus from the grave.

Some translations of this verse say "Deliver us from the evil one." That view places evil outside us. The perception of external evil has existed since the earliest of days.

"Sin is crouching at your door;
it desires to have you,
but you must rule over it."

GENESIS 4:7

While the evil one is recognized as powerful and capable of overpowering us, when we are by ourselves, our comfort and assurance is that we are not alone. And there is one more powerful than the evil one who is on our side.

"Because greater is he that is in you,
than he that is in the world."

1 JOHN 4:4 KJV

When God told Abraham and Sarah that Sarah would have a child by Abraham, they found it hard to believe. Abraham was almost a hundred years old and Sarah was ninety years old.

God posed a question to them:

"Is anything too hard for the Lord?"

GENESIS 18:14 NIV

God presented the same question to Jeremiah as He gave him the prophetic vision regarding the nation of Israel whose people were about to be taken captive, while also promising to bring them back from captivity in Babylon.

"I am the Lord,

the God of all mankind.

Is anything too hard for me?"

JEREMIAH 32:26

Figuratively, that is the miracle that God performs in each of us when He becomes the one to whom we resonate! He rescues us and brings us home from the worldly "Babylon" that takes us captive.[39]

CHAPTER 9

DOXOLOGY

FOR YOURS IS THE KINGDOM, THE POWER AND GLORY, FOREVER. AMEN.

D oxologies are brief praises to God, usually sung or recited at the end of a prayer. In this doxology, we hear
echoes of King David giving thanks to God on the last
day of his reign over Israel:

"Yours, Lord,
is the greatness and the power
and the glory and the majesty
and the splendor,
for everything in heaven
and earth is yours!
Yours, Lord, is the kingdom;
you are exalted as head over all."

1 CHRONICLES 29:11 NIV

Significantly, King David stated this in the assembly of the
commanders of his army, the officials of his palace, his family,
and all the prominent people of the kingdom, as he voluntarily
handed over his kingdom to Solomon, "Son of David." How
interesting that we, too, offer this doxology as we voluntarily

hand over our respective kingdoms to our Lord Jesus, who is also referred to as "Son of David."

The message of Jesus, in all his teachings, was the good news of the Kingdom of God, his Father, being available to all who would wish to have it through his substitutionary sacrifice. The kingdom of course belongs to the Father. We are adopted into His family and made heirs of that kingdom. We are reminded here that it has happened entirely by His power and not by anything we have done besides our acceptance of what He has offered. The glory, therefore, belongs entirely to Him as well.

Celebratory fireworks provide imagery depicting glory. On Independence Day, the final burst of fireworks is usually awe inspiring and caps the celebratory tribute. In our case, in this verse, we offer the highest form of imaginable glory to mark the celebration of the converse: our "Dependence Days." Following the end of the fireworks on Independence Day is usually a lull and dispersal. But the glory offered to our Father is endless, going on forever and ever.

For any system to function, it has to be powered. We recognize the power of God, which was best displayed in the resurrection of Jesus! It is his resurrection that puts his message into context and lends credence to the gospel message of the Father's Kingdom being available to us. Throughout the ages, death has been man's greatest fear. Jesus overcame death by God's power and assures us that we can too. While that same power is available to us, there is no doubt as to whom that power belongs. Yours, O Lord, is the power. Since we now belong to Your family, we too get the benefit of Your power!

The previous verse ended with us asking for deliverance from evil. We now have the identity of the "delivered one." From the vantage point of the delivered, we recognize that we have deliverance into the Kingdom of Heaven. Whose kingdom is that? It is our Father's Kingdom, introduced to us by Jesus, our deliverer. We have access to His Kingdom because we were adopted into His family when we believed that Jesus came as the son of the Father with the express purpose of redeeming us into our Father's Kingdom. Let us behold our deliverer. He is referred to as the Lord, Savior, Messiah, or Christ.

Jesus accepted being incarnate in lowly, humble form: that of a helpless baby, seemingly conceived by a poor un-wed couple, born unhoused in a land under brutal occupation. We are told that, as an infant, he was a refugee, shielded by his parents from those who sought his destruction. The little that is written about his childhood is about his passion for his heavenly Father's house. As an adult, he assembled a crew of a dozen ordinary, previously undistinguished men, whom he taught to take his message all over the world. Part of what Jesus taught them was the prayer we have just studied.

Jesus's main message was that his Father's Kingdom of Heaven was available to everyone. He drew attention to the awareness that man had gone astray but, more importantly, that there was a way back. He was and *is* the way!

After teaching his followers the approved way to live, He willingly offered his life on the cross as the ransom price for mankind: the sacrifice of the pure to enable the impure to be redeemed, sanctified, and delivered into his Father's Kingdom. He bridged our world of matter and the metaphysical world of his Father's Kingdom. He overcame death, having experienced it himself, but he transcended it by rising up from the grave, and he now lives beyond it. He invites us all to follow him into the Kingdom of his Father and not perish at the point of earthly death. In the process, we get sanctified and transformed into disciples.

Discipleship has its privilege, but it also has its cost. And that cost could even be death, here on earth. But as Jim Elliott, the young missionary who was martyred in Ecuador, so powerfully stated,

"He is no fool who
gives what he cannot keep,
to gain what he cannot lose." [40]

Jesus urges us not to be fearful of death nor of the challenges we face while we live here, because he (his Spirit) will lead and guide us.

"In this world, you will have trouble.
But take heart!
I have overcome the world."

JOHN 16:33

Jesus undertakes to provide the direction as well as the power. He will not send us where he has not been. His expectation of each of us who wish to be his disciple is very simple: **"Follow me."**

Jesus and his (our) Father are one. Hence, our heartfelt adulation:

"Yours is the kingdom,
the power and glory, forever.
Amen."

RECAP

In the Introduction, we had stated that, through this prayer, Jesus taught both the gospel message as well as the process of sanctification. Let us look back over the prayer to see if we grasped those treasures.

Jesus's gospel message was that he had come to make his Father's (God's) Kingdom of Heaven accessible to anyone who chose to accept that offer. But Jesus would be the only way to his Father's Kingdom. When we accept his offer, we receive a new identity as members of his Father's family, as well as permanent citizenship in Heaven. Our salvation provides us a new destiny, avoiding perdition whenever we happen to die on earth. All of us who are adopted into Jesus's and his Father's family will also have the continuous presence alongside us of the Holy Spirit, who is the helper and counselor sent by our Father and serves as our interface with Him. That in itself would be a plentiful harvest reaped from this prayer. But there's more.

The remainder of the prayer takes us along the sanctification process that changes us from who we were to becoming more like Jesus, which is every disciple's goal. Jesus always exalted his Father. We are also to always revere and honor the name of our Father. How thrilling that we now have His name too!

Now that we are members of God's family and His Kingdom, our lives on earth are extensions of His Kingdom too. We get to experience Heaven metaphysically when we accept our Father's presence, His sovereignty, and yield totally to His will, guided by the Holy Spirit. We prioritize His Kingdom as we surrender our will and our respective kingdoms to Him to manage as His.

We will feed on the sustenance provided us by our Father, accepting our dependence on Him. We acknowledge Jesus as the bread that came down from Heaven and feed on his word and his body broken for us—that we may also be willing to be broken, in His service, at His direction. He is the stem cell that restores our soul. We confidently seek forgiveness for our trespasses and debts, knowing that Jesus fully paid the price for our forgiveness on the cross. Having received His mercy and grace, we likewise extend mercy and grace to others, including those who may have hurt us badly, always remembering how Jesus forgave the ones who mercilessly crucified him, even while they did so.

Though cleansed and forgiven, we recognize our vulnerability because we still have to make all the decisions and choices in our life. We acknowledge we are at risk of giving in to the temptations that bombard us and lure us in the ways of the world. We are mindful that our former temptations lie dormant like land mines, capable of being reactivated and derailing us. We seek the continual reorientation of our spirit directed by the Holy Spirit and beseech our Father to deliver us from the evil that still lurks within us.

We have the continuous presence of the same enduring Spirit, who was in Jesus and raised him from death, to guide and counsel us. We are assured of deliverance into His Kingdom by His power, for which we glorify God our Father, Jesus our savior, and the Holy Spirit who guides us, forever.

Each time we immerse ourselves in this prayer, we relive the joy of our salvation and get further refined by the sanctification it effects. We get to become a little more like Jesus.

Certainly, there is no greater treasure available to man, and we have been provided access to it.

That calls for a Hallelujah!

REFERENCES

The Bible quotations in this book are from the New International Version unless stated otherwise.

1. David A. Moses et al, "Neuroprosthesis for Decoding Speech in a Paralyzed Person with Anarthria," *New England Journal of Medicine* (2021); 385:217–227, https://doi: 10.1056/NEJMoa2027540.

2. William Paley, *Natural Theology: or, Evidences of the Existence and Attributes of the Deity* (London: R Faulder; Philadelphia: John Morgan, 1802), 6.

3. John Owen, Kelly Kapic, and Justin Taylor, eds., *Communion with the Triune God* (Wheaton, IL: Crossway, 2007), 152–212.

4. J. D. Watson and F. H. C. Crick, "A Structure for Deoxyribose Nucleic Acid," *Nature* (April 1953); 171:737–738, https://doi.org/10.1038/171737a0.

5. Ira D. Sankey, "Blessed Assurance" – *My Life and the Story of the Gospel Hymns* (Philadelphia: *Sunday School Times*, 1906), 136 –139.

6. Leo Burnett and Studio M, "McDonald's 'Swing,'" YouTube video, :30, Nov 1, 2013, https://www.youtube.com/watch?v=4MGI-EJQtgo.

7. *Jeopardy!*, season 39, episode 197, "Show #8827," directed by Lucinda Ireland, aired June 13, 2023, CBS Media Ventures.

8. "Mahatma Gandhi Says He Believes in Christ But Not Christianity," *The Harvard Crimson*, January 11, 1927, https://www.thecrimson.com/article/1927/1/11/mahatma-gandhi-says-he-believes-in/.

9. "Have Thine Own Way, Lord," Hymnary.org, https://hymnary.org/text/have_thine_own_way_lord.

10. Craig Groeschel, *The Christian Atheist: Believing in God but Living as if He Doesn't Exist* (Grand Rapids, MI: Zondervan, 2011), 14.

11. Andrew Murray, *Absolute Surrender* (Abbottsford, MI: Aneko Press Christian Classics, 2017), 38.

12. Richard Carlson, *Don't Sweat the Small Stuff . . . and It's All Small Stuff* (Alcoa, TN: Fine Communications, 1997), 61.

13. C S Lewis, *The Great Divorce* (Springfield, OH: Collier Books, 1978), 71.

14. "Maranatha—Our Lord, Come," Precept Austin, https://www.preceptaustin.org/maranatha.

15. Andrew Messner, "*Maranatha* (1 Corinthians 16:22): Reconstruction and Translation Based on Western Middle Aramaic," *Journal of Biblical Literature* (2020); 139(2):361–383, https://doi.org/10.15699/jbl.1392.2020.7.

16. The Editors of *Encyclopedia Britannica*, "Didache," last updated October 18, 2021, https://www.britannica.com/topic/Didache.

17. Michelle Baddeley, "Keynes' Psychology and Behavioural Microeconomics: Theory and Policy," *The Economic and Labour Relations Review* (2017); 28(1538):1035304617706849, https://doi.org/10.1177/1035304617706849.

18. "GPS: The Global Positioning System," National Coordination Office for Space-Based Positioning, Navigation, and Timing, last modified July 10, 2023, https://www.gps.gov.

19. The Editors of *Encyclopedia Britannica*, s.v. "Servomechanism," last modified January 29, 1999, https://www.britannica.com/technology/servomechanism/additional-info#history.

20. William Shakespeare, *As You Like It*, Jack Randall Crawford, ed. (New Haven, CT: Yale University Press, 1919), 61.

21. Charles Haddon Spurgeon, *Scripture: Matthew 6:13*, in *The Metropolitan Tabernacle Pulpit, Vol. 24: Sermons Preached and Revised by C. H. Spurgeon, During the Year 1878* – Classic Reprint (London: Forgotten Books, 2018). 61.

22. Bible Hub, Berean Literal Bible, "Matthew 6:11" (No location: Berean Standard Bible Press, 2021), https://biblehub.com/matthew/6-11.htm.

23. George Muller, "Trusting God for Daily Bread," https://harvestministry.org/muller#:~:text=George%20M%C3%BCller%20(1805%2D1898),for%20over%20120%2C000%20orphan%20children.

24. T. C. E. Cheng and S. Podolsky, *Just-in-Time Manufacturing: An Introduction*, 2nd ed. (London: Chapman and Hall, 1993), 1–32.

25. Dan, Rudge, "Foreshadows of Christ and Calvary: A Typical Provision (Exodus 16), Truth & Tidings (June 2019); 70:6, https://truthandtidings.com/2019/06/foreshadows-of-christ-and-calvary-a-typical-provision-exodus-16/.

26. J. Brillat-Savarin (2008a), *Philosophical History of Cooking*. In David Inglis, Debra Gimlin, and Chris Thorpe (eds.), *Food: Critical Concepts in Social Sciences*, Vol. 1 (London/New York: Rutledge, 2007), 93–110.

27.   RM Aly, "Current State of Stem Cell Based Therapies: An Overview," *Stem Cell Investigation*, 2020 May 15: 7:8–8, https://doi: 10:21037/sci-2020-001.

28.   William Tyndale, *New Testament – Romans to Revelation* (Worms, Germany: Press of Peter Schoeffer, 1526).

29.   *The Book of Common Prayer* (New York: Church Publishing, 1979). 85.

30.   *The Lion King*, directed by Roger Allers and Rob Minkoff (Burbank, CA: Walt Disney Pictures and Walt Disney Feature Animation), DVD.

31.   Former President Bill Clinton, interview by Dan Rather, *60 Minutes*, CBS, June 20, 2004.

32.   *Cambridge Dictionary*, s.v. "Outpost," https://dictionary.cambridge.org.

33.   Charles M. Sheldon, *In His Steps: What Would Jesus Do?* (Ada, MI: Revell, 1985), 21.

34.   N. D. Weinstein, "Unrealistic Optimism about Future Life Events," *Journal of Personality and Social Psychology*, 39, no. 5 (1980), 806–820, https://doi.org/10.1037/0022-3514.39.5.806.

35.   Tali Sharot, *The Optimism Bias: A Tour of the Irrationally Positive Brain*, Reprint ed. (New York: Vintage, 2012), 40–59.

36.   I Am Second, https://iamsecond.com.

37. Matt Jenkins, "Steering Ships through a Treacherous Waterway," *Smithsonian Magazine*, February 2009, https://www.smithsonianmag.com/science-nature/steering-ships-through-a-treacherous-waterway-45259458/.

38. Alcoholics Anonymous World Services, Inc., *Twelve Steps and Twelve Traditions* (New York, 1981), 21–24.

39. "The Meaning of 'Babylon,'" Early Church History, https://earlychurchhistory.org/politics/the-meaning-of-babylon/.

40. Elizabeth Elliott, ed., *The Journals of Jim Elliott* (Grand Rapids, MI: 2002). 106.

OUR FATHER

DISCOVER THE MAP TO THE GREATEST TREASURE

GEORGE MATHEWS, MD